(WeightWatchers®
PointsPlus⊕

I ❤ LEFTOVERS

**Tuscan-Style Beef Roast
with Fennel and Olives, 18**

WeightWatchers®
PointsPlus⊕

I ♥ LEFTOVERS

175+ DELICIOUS RECIPES
TO SERVE NOW OR LATER

Leg of Lamb Infused with Rosemary and Lemon, 93, and Minted Green Beans with Pine Nuts, 37

About

WeightWatchers®

Weight Watchers International, Inc. is the world's leading provider of weight-management services, operating globally through a network of company-owned and franchise operations. Weight Watchers holds nearly 50,000 weekly meetings worldwide, at which members receive group support and education about healthful eating patterns, behavior modification, and physical activity. Weight-loss and weight-management results vary by individual. We recommend that you attend Weight Watchers meetings to benefit from the supportive environment you find there and follow the comprehensive Weight Watchers program, which includes a food plan, an activity plan, and a behavioral component. In addition, Weight Watchers offers a wide range of products, publications, and programs for people interested in weight loss and weight control. For the Weight Watchers meeting nearest you, call **1–800–651–6000**. For information about bringing Weight Watchers to your workplace, call **1–800-8AT-WORK.**

Also visit us at our Web site, **WeightWatchers.com**, and look for **Weight Watchers Magazine** at your newsstand or in your meeting room.

Weight Watchers Publishing Group

VP, Editorial Director **Nancy Gagliardi**

Creative Director **Ed Melnitsky**

Photo Director **Deborah Hardt**

Managing Editor **Diane Pavia**

Assistant Editor **Katerina Gkionis**

Food Editor **Eileen Runyan**

Editor **Jackie Mills, R.D.**

Recipe Developers **Adrienne Anderson, Jean Galton, Maureen Luchejko, Jackie Plant**

Production Manager **Alan Biederman**

Photographer **Kate Mathis**

Food Stylist **Adrienne Anderson**

Prop Stylist **Marcus Hay**

Art Director **LeAnna Weller Smith**

Designer **Gary Tooth, Empire Design Studio**

SKU #11981 Printed in the USA

FRONT COVER: From top left:
Fiery Chili Chicken Legs, page 50; Grilled Vegetable–Pesto Pizza, page 209; Leg of Lamb Infused with Rosemary and Lemon, page 93; Argentine-Style Flank Steak Stuffed with Spinach, page 77; Mini–Chocolate Cheesecakes, page 142; Turkey-Succotash Potpie with Crispy Phyllo Crust, page 55.

BACK COVER: Indian-Spiced Grilled Turkey Pitas, page 194.

Contents

Grilled Vegetable–Pesto
Pizza, 209

About Our Recipes

While losing weight isn't only about what you eat, Weight Watchers realizes the critical role it plays in your success and overall good health. That's why our philosophy is to offer great-tasting, easy recipes that are nutritious as well as delicious. We make every attempt to use wholesome ingredients and to ensure that our recipes fall within the recommendations of the U.S. Dietary Guidelines for Americans for a diet that promotes health and reduces the risk for disease. If you have special dietary needs, consult with your health-care professional for advice on a diet that is best for you, then adapt these recipes to meet your specific nutritional needs.

To achieve these good-health goals and get the maximum satisfaction from the foods you eat, we suggest you keep the following information in mind while preparing our recipes:

The Program and Good Nutrition

Recipes in this book have been developed for Weight Watchers members who are following the *PointsPlus*® program. *PointsPlus* values are given for each recipe. They're calculated based on the amount of protein, carbohydrates, fat, and fiber contained in a single serving of a recipe.

● Recipes include approximate nutritional information; they are analyzed for Calories (Cal), Total Fat, Saturated Fat (Sat Fat), Trans Fat, Cholesterol (Chol), Sodium (Sod), Carbohydrates (Carb), Sugar, Dietary Fiber (Fib), Protein (Prot), and Calcium (Calc). The nutritional values are calculated by registered dietitians, using nutrition analysis software.

● Substitutions made to the ingredients will alter the per-serving nutritional information and may affect the *PointsPlus* value.

● Our recipes meet Weight Watchers Good Health Guidelines for eating lean proteins and fiber-rich whole grains, and having at least five servings of vegetables and fruits and two servings of low-fat or fat-free dairy products a day, while limiting your intake of saturated fat, sugar, and sodium.

● Health agencies recommend limiting sodium intake. To stay in line with this recommendation we keep sodium levels in our recipes reasonably low; to boost flavor, we often include fresh herbs or a squeeze of citrus instead of salt. If you don't have to restrict your sodium, feel free to add a touch more salt as desired.

● In the recipes, a green triangle (▲) indicates Weight Watchers® Power Foods.

● FOR YOUR INFO serving suggestions have a **PointsPlus** value of 0 unless otherwise stated.

● Recipes that work with the Simply Filling technique are listed on page 213. Find more details about this technique at your meeting.

For additional information about the science behind lasting weight loss and more, please visit **WeightWatchers.com/science.**

All **PointsPlus** values in this book are for one serving.

Calculations not what you expected?

● You might expect some of the **PointsPlus** values in this book to be lower when some of the foods they're made from, such as fruits and vegetables, have no **PointsPlus** values. Most fruits and veggies have no **PointsPlus** values when served as a snack or part of a meal, like a cup of berries with a sandwich. But if these foods are part of a recipe, their fiber and nutrient content are incorporated into the recipe calculations. These nutrients can affect the **PointsPlus** values.

● Alcohol is included in our **PointsPlus** calculations. Because alcohol information is generally not included on nutrition labels, it's not an option to include when using the hand calculator or the online calculator. But since we use alcohol information that we get from our nutritionists you might notice discrepancies between the **PointsPlus** values you see in our recipes and the values you get using the calculator. The **PointsPlus** values listed for our recipes are the most accurate values.

Shopping for Ingredients

As you learn to eat healthier and add more Weight Watchers Power Foods to your meals, remember these tips for choosing foods wisely:

Lean Meats and Poultry Purchase lean meats and poultry, and trim them of all visible fat before cooking. When poultry is cooked with the skin on, we recommend removing the skin before eating. Nutritional information for recipes that include meat, poultry, and fish is based on cooked, skinless boneless portions (unless otherwise stated), with the fat trimmed.

Seafood Whenever possible, our recipes call for seafood that is sustainable and deemed the most healthful for human consumption so that your choice of seafood is not only good for the oceans but also good for you. For more information about how to make the best seafood choices and to download a pocket guide, go to **environmentaldefensefund.org** or **montereybayaquarium.org.** For information about mercury levels and seafood go to **WeightWatchers.com.**

Produce For best flavor, maximum nutrient content, and the lowest prices, buy fresh, local produce, such as vegetables, leafy greens, and fruits in season. Rinse them thoroughly before using and keep a supply of cut-up vegetables and fruits in your refrigerator for convenient, healthy snacks.

Whole Grains Explore your market for whole-grain products such as whole wheat and whole-grain breads and pastas, brown rice, bulgur, barley, cornmeal, whole wheat couscous, oats, and quinoa to enjoy with your meals.

Preparation and Measuring

Read the Recipe Take a couple of minutes to read through the ingredients and directions before you start to prepare a recipe. This will prevent you from discovering midway through that you don't have an important ingredient or that a recipe requires several hours of marinating. And it's also a good idea to assemble all ingredients and utensils within easy reach before you begin a recipe.

Weighing and Measuring The success of any recipe depends on accurate weighing and measuring. The effectiveness of the Weight Watchers program and the accuracy of the nutritional analysis depend on correct measuring as well. Use the following techniques:

- Weigh food such as meat, poultry, and fish on a food scale.

- To measure liquids, use a standard glass or plastic measuring cup placed on a level surface. For amounts less than $1/4$ cup, use standard measuring spoons.

- To measure dry ingredients, use metal or plastic measuring cups that come in $1/4$-, $1/3$-, $1/2$-, and 1-cup sizes. Fill the appropriate cup and level it with the flat edge of a knife or spatula. For amounts less than $1/4$ cup, use standard measuring spoons.

Recipe Symbol 🕐 20 minutes or less

Make-Ahead Smarts

Preparing meals in advance and planning for leftovers is a real life-saver on busy nights when you don't have the time or energy to cook. It's important to follow a few rules when it comes to advance meal prep so that meals are as delicious as when they were first prepared. Follow these tips for making sure the food you make ahead is fresh tasting and safe to eat.

Before You Store

Cook food until it is at a safe temperature. Don't partially cook meat or poultry with the intention of fully cooking when you reheat, since bacteria can grow unless food is fully cooked at the start. For beef, pork, and lamb steaks, chops, and roasts, cook to an internal temperature of 145°F; for ground beef, pork and lamb, cook to an internal temperature of 160°F. All poultry should be cooked to an internal temperature of 165°F.

Cool food quickly. To speed up cooling, transfer large batches of foods such as soups or stews to a large shallow container or to several smaller containers and allow to stand at room temperature until cool, no longer than 2 hours. Alternatively, place the container of food in an ice bath and allow to cool before refrigerating. Monitor the food carefully and refrigerate or freeze the food as soon as it is cool.

Storage Know-How

Choose containers that work best for you. Glass or plastic containers are inexpensive, have a tight seal, and come in space-saving stackable designs. Shallow containers are the best choice because they allow food to cool faster. Zip-close plastic bags are also inexpensive and do a great job of keeping food fresh. Once frozen, the bags can either lay flat or stack on their sides. Vacuum seal systems are costly, but convenient to use and keep more air away from your food, allowing it to remain fresher longer than with ordinary containers or zip-close plastic bags.

Portion foods for how you'll use them. If you'll be reheating four servings for a family meal, put the food in one large container. If the food is for lunches you'll have at work, store it in single-serve containers. Choose freezer containers that have a maximum capacity of 1 quart to ensure that the food will freeze rapidly. For cakes and other baked goods that you plan to serve whole, wrap and freeze the whole cake; if you'll be enjoying individual slices as afternoon snacks, cut the cake into slices and freeze them individually.

Label and date the packages. Whichever food storage system you use, be sure to label the food to identify the item and the date that you froze or stored it. Use freezer tape, which is specially designed to adhere in cold moist conditions. For zip-close plastic bags, use a permanent marker to write on the bag itself.

Wrap baked goods well for storage. Always let baked goods cool completely before storing or freezing. For small items such as muffins or scones, place them in a zip-close plastic freezer bag, squeeze out as much air as possible, seal, and freeze. For foods such as loaf breads or cakes, wrap them tightly in plastic wrap, then in heavy-duty foil and freeze.

Cover or seal the food. Leave as little air as possible in the container so foods will remain moist and fresh tasting. A tight seal helps prevent freezer burn and keeps odors from the food from permeating other foods in the refrigerator or freezer. When freezing liquid foods such as soups or stews, leave some headspace in the container, since the food will expand slightly as it freezes.

How long will it keep? Use the chart below to determine how long to keep precooked refrigerated or frozen foods. Frozen food will be safe to eat for a month or two longer than indicated in the chart, but these recommended times will insure the best flavor and quality.

Recommended Storage Times for Cooked Foods

Type of Food	Refrigerated	Frozen
Beef, pork, lamb	3–4 days	2–3 months
Poultry	3–4 days	4 months
Seafood	3–4 days	2–3 months
Egg dishes	3–4 days	2–3 months
Soups, stews, casseroles	3–4 days	2–3 months
Baked goods	Not recommended	2–3 months

Thawing 101

Plan ahead. The safest way to thaw food is in the refrigerator. Portions of most foods to serve up to four people will thaw overnight (or while you're at work) in the refrigerator. Baked goods, such as muffins, scones, or cakes, can be thawed at room temperature, or if you're reheating a single serving, they can go from the freezer to the microwave for reheating.

You have other options. If you forget to thaw food in the refrigerator, you can defrost it in cold water if it is in an airtight container or a sealed zip-close plastic bag. Submerge the food in cold water, changing the water every 30 minutes, until the food is thawed. You can also use your microwave's defrost setting to thaw food, but watch the food carefully so that it does not begin to cook during the defrost cycle. Once food is thawed in cold water or in the microwave, cook it immediately.

Thaw, heat, and eat. Once food is thawed, don't refreeze it; reheat it thoroughly and serve it immediately. Although it's safe to eat if it's frozen again, the quality will deteriorate.

Reheating Recommendations

Heat foods until hot. Reheat precooked foods to 165°F, whether reheating on the stovetop, in the oven, or in the microwave. Use a thermometer to check the temperature in the center of casseroles and bring soups and stews to a full boil before serving.

Don't reheat in a slow cooker. Because food may be at an unsafe temperature for too long before it gets hot, reheating in a slow cooker is not recommended. But, you can reheat the food on the stovetop or microwave and put it in a preheated slow cooker to keep it hot for serving.

Any doubt? Throw it out. If you're not sure how long food has been refrigerated, it's safest to discard it. Harmful bacteria cannot be detected by the look or smell of food; it may look and smell acceptable, but be harmful to eat.

Now or Later
Main Dishes

Make these hearty entrees and enjoy them as soon as they're ready, or follow the instructions with each recipe for storing, reheating, and serving later. Either way, you'll serve your family a delicious home cooked meal with little fuss.

Tuscan-Style Beef Roast with Fennel and Olives Serves 6

▲ 1 **(1 1/2-pound) boneless lean bottom round roast, trimmed**

3/4 **teaspoon salt**

1/2 **teaspoon pepper**

2 **teaspoons olive oil**

▲ 2 **leeks, cleaned and sliced, white and light green parts only**

▲ 1 **fennel bulb, halved and sliced crosswise**

3 **garlic cloves, coarsely chopped**

▲ 1 **(28-ounce) can whole peeled tomatoes**

1 **cup dry red wine**

1/2 **cup water**

12 **oil-cured black olives, pitted and chopped**

1 **tablespoon chopped fresh rosemary**

1 Preheat oven to 350°F.

2 Sprinkle beef with 1/2 teaspoon salt and pepper. Heat oil in Dutch oven over medium-high heat. Add beef and cook, turning frequently, until browned, about 8 minutes. Transfer beef to plate.

3 Add leeks, fennel, and garlic, and cook, stirring occasionally, until vegetables are tender, about 8 minutes. Add tomatoes, wine, water, olives, rosemary, and remaining 1/4 teaspoon salt. Return beef and any accumulated juices to Dutch oven; cover and bring to simmer. Transfer Dutch oven to oven and bake until beef is fork-tender, about 1 hour 45 minutes. Cut beef across grain into 12 slices. Serve with sauce.

Per serving (2 slices beef with 1/2 cup sauce): 298 Cal, 9 g Total Fat, 3 g Sat Fat, 0 g Trans Fat, 88 mg Chol, 716 mg Sod, 15 g Carb, 5 g Sugar, 3 g Fib, 31 g Prot, 81 mg Calc.

STORE AND SERVE LATER

Transfer beef slices and sauce to an airtight container and let cool. Cover and refrigerate up to 4 days or freeze up to 3 months. To reheat, if frozen, thaw the beef and sauce in the refrigerator overnight. Transfer to a large skillet. Cover and cook over medium heat until heated through, 8–10 minutes.

Pairs Well With: Polenta with Goat Cheese and Chives, page 181

**Tuscan-Style Beef Roast
with Fennel and Olives**

Steak Roulade Stuffed with Mushrooms and Spinach Serves 4

2 teaspoons olive oil

▲ 3/4 pound shiitake mushrooms, stems discarded and caps sliced

3 garlic cloves, minced

▲ 1 (5-ounce) container baby spinach

3 tablespoons whole wheat bread crumbs

▲ 1 (1-pound) lean flank steak, trimmed

1/2 teaspoon salt

1/4 teaspoon pepper

▲ 2 Vidalia or other sweet onions, thinly sliced

▲ 3/4 cup reduced-sodium beef broth

1/2 cup dry red wine

1 tablespoon chopped fresh thyme

1 tablespoon all-purpose flour

2 tablespoons water

1 To make filling, heat 1 teaspoon oil in large skillet over medium-high heat. Add mushrooms and garlic and cook, stirring occasionally, until mushrooms are tender, about 8 minutes. Stir in spinach and cook until wilted, about 2 minutes. Transfer to medium bowl; stir in bread crumbs. Let cool slightly.

2 Place steak on cutting board. Starting at one long side, cut steak three-quarters of way through, leaving a 1/2-inch hinge, and open up steak like a book. Sprinkle steak with salt and pepper. Spoon filling over steak leaving 1/2-inch border. From one short end, roll up jelly-roll fashion. Tie with kitchen string at 1-inch intervals.

3 Heat remaining 1 teaspoon oil in Dutch oven over medium-high heat. Add roulade and cook until browned on all sides, 5 minutes. Add onions, broth, wine, and thyme; bring to boil. Simmer, covered, until fork-tender, about 1 1/2 hours. Transfer to cutting board. Let rest 5 minutes.

4 Meanwhile, whisk together flour and water in small bowl until smooth. Add flour mixture to onion mixture, whisking constantly. Simmer, stirring constantly, until sauce is thickened, 3–4 minutes. Cut roulade into 8 slices and serve with sauce.

Per serving (2 slices roulade and 1/3 cup sauce): 357 Cal, 10 g Total Fat, 3 g Sat Fat, 0 g Trans Fat, 42 mg Chol, 498 mg Sod, 35 g Carb, 12 g Sugar, 5 g Fib, 29 g Prot, 101 mg Calc.

STORE AND SERVE LATER

Prepare the roulade and sauce, but do not slice the roulade. Transfer to an airtight container and let cool. Cover and refrigerate up to 4 days or freeze up to 3 months. To reheat, if frozen, thaw the roulade and sauce in the refrigerator overnight. Transfer to a large skillet. Cover and cook over medium heat, stirring the sauce occasionally, until heated through, 15–20 minutes. Slice the roulade and serve with the sauce.

Braised Beef Braciola with Parmesan and Pine Nuts Serves 4

¼ cup whole wheat bread crumbs

▲ 1 large hard-cooked egg, coarsely chopped

3 tablespoons chopped fresh parsley

2 tablespoons grated Parmesan cheese

2 tablespoons toasted pine nuts

1 tablespoon capers, drained

2 teaspoons dry vermouth or water

▲ 4 (¼-inch-thick) slices lean top round steak, trimmed (3 ounces each)

2 slices prosciutto (about 1 ounce), each slice cut lengthwise in half

2 teaspoons olive oil

▲ 1 (14½-ounce) can diced tomatoes

3 garlic cloves, minced

3 tablespoons chopped fresh basil

1 To make filling, combine bread crumbs, egg, parsley, cheese, pine nuts, capers, and vermouth in medium bowl until well mixed.

2 Place 1 steak between 2 sheets of wax paper. Pound steak to ⅛-inch thickness. Repeat with remaining steaks. Remove and discard top sheets of wax paper. Place 1 prosciutto slice on each steak. Press about 2 tablespoons filling onto each steak, leaving ½-inch border. From one short end, roll up each steak jelly-roll fashion. Tie each roll at 1-inch intervals with kitchen string.

3 Heat oil in large skillet over medium-high heat. Add rolls and cook, turning occasionally, until browned, 3–4 minutes. Add tomatoes and garlic; bring to boil. Reduce heat and simmer, covered, until braciola is fork-tender, 1 ½ hours. Stir in basil.

Per serving (1 braciola with ¼ cup sauce): 276 Cal, 12 g Total Fat, 3 g Sat Fat, 0 g Trans Fat, 103 mg Chol, 687 mg Sod, 11 g Carb, 4 g Sugar, 2 g Fib, 27 g Prot, 86 mg Calc.

STORE AND SERVE LATER
Transfer braciola and sauce to an airtight container and let cool. Cover and refrigerate up to 4 days or freeze up to 3 months. To reheat, if frozen, thaw the braciola and sauce in the refrigerator overnight. Transfer to a large skillet. Cover and cook over medium heat, stirring occasionally, until heated through, 15–20 minutes.

Pairs Well With: Herbed Parmesan-Garlic Pasta, page 181

Belgian Beef and Dark Beer Stew Serves 4

2	teaspoons canola oil
▲ 1	pound boneless lean sirloin steak, trimmed and cut into 1-inch cubes
▲ 2	onions, chopped
1	tablespoon all-purpose flour
1	(12-ounce) bottle dark beer
▲ 1	cup reduced-sodium beef broth
1	tablespoon red currant jelly
2	teaspoons apple cider vinegar
4	fresh thyme sprigs
1/2	teaspoon salt
▲ 1 1/2	cups baby carrots

1 Heat oil in Dutch oven over medium-high heat. Add beef and cook, stirring occasionally, until browned, about 6 minutes. Transfer beef to plate.

2 Add onions to Dutch oven and cook, stirring occasionally, until onions are softened, about 8 minutes. Add flour, and cook, stirring constantly, 1 minute. Add beer, broth, jelly, vinegar, thyme, and salt; bring to boil. Return beef and any accumulated juices to Dutch oven. Cover and simmer, stirring occasionally, until beef is just tender. Remove and discard thyme sprigs.

3 Add carrots and cook until beef and vegetables are fork-tender, about 15 minutes.

Per serving (1 cup): 276 Cal, 7 g Total Fat, 2 g Sat Fat, 0 g Trans Fat, 49 mg Chol, 378 mg Sod, 19 g Carb, 10 g Sugar, 3 g Fib, 28 g Prot, 48 mg Calc.

6 PointsPlus® value

STORE AND SERVE LATER
Prepare the stew through step 2. Transfer to an airtight container and let cool. Cover and refrigerate up to 4 days or freeze up to 3 months. To reheat, if frozen, thaw the stew in the refrigerator overnight. Transfer to a large saucepan. Add the carrots and cook as directed in step 3.

Pairs Well With: Arugula and Parmesan Salad, page 87

Beef, Wild Mushroom, and Bean Stew Serves 6

2 teaspoons canola oil

▲ 1 pound lean top round steak, trimmed and cut into 1-inch cubes

▲ 1 (8-ounce) package mixed wild mushrooms, halved if large

▲ 1 onion, finely chopped

▲ 1 red bell pepper, diced

2 garlic cloves, minced

1 tablespoon tomato paste

▲ 3 cups reduced-sodium beef broth

▲ 2 (15 1/2-ounce) can pinto beans, rinsed and drained

1/4 teaspoon salt

▲ 1/2 pound green beans, trimmed and cut into 1-inch pieces

1 Heat oil in large saucepan over medium-high heat. Add beef and cook, turning occasionally, until browned, about 6 minutes. Transfer beef to plate.

2 Add mushrooms, onion, bell pepper, and garlic to saucepan and cook over medium heat, stirring occasionally, until vegetables are softened, about 8 minutes. Add tomato paste, stirring until blended. Add broth, pinto beans, and salt; bring to boil. Cover and simmer, stirring occasionally, until beef is fork-tender, about 1 hour.

3 Add green beans to saucepan and cook, stirring occasionally, until beans are crisp-tender, 3–4 minutes.

Per serving (1 1/3 cups): 297 Cal, 6 g Total Fat, 1 g Sat Fat, 0 g Trans Fat, 37 mg Chol, 623 mg Sod, 29 g Carb, 3 g Sugar, 9 g Fib, 29 g Prot, 80 mg Calc.

STORE AND SERVE LATER

Prepare the stew through step 2. Transfer to an airtight container and let cool. Cover and refrigerate up to 4 days or freeze up to 3 months. To reheat, if frozen, thaw the stew in the refrigerator overnight. Transfer to a medium saucepan. Cover and cook over medium heat, stirring occasionally, until heated through, 8–10 minutes. Add the green beans and cook as directed in step 3.

Sauerbraten-Style Meatloaf with Gingersnap–Apple Sauce and Buttered Broccoli with Lemon and Parmesan, 36

Sauerbraten-Style Meatloaf with Gingersnap–Apple Sauce Serves 6

2 teaspoons canola oil

▲ 1 onion, chopped

▲ 1 Granny Smith apple, peeled, cored, and diced

4 reduced-fat gingersnap cookies, coarsely crushed

▲ 1½ pounds lean ground beef (7% fat or less)

½ cup whole wheat bread crumbs

¼ cup ketchup

▲ 1 large egg, lightly beaten

½ teaspoon salt

▲ 1 cup reduced-sodium chicken broth

¼ cup unsweetened apple juice

2 teaspoons cornstarch

1 Preheat oven to 350°F. Spray 4 x 8-inch loaf pan with nonstick spray.

2 Heat oil in large nonstick skillet over medium-high heat. Add onion and apple and cook, stirring occasionally, until tender, 10 minutes. Add gingersnaps and cook, until cookies begin to dissolve, 3–4 minutes.

3 Transfer half of the onion mixture to large bowl; reserve remaining onion mixture in skillet. Let onion mixture in bowl cool slightly. Add beef, bread crumbs, ketchup, egg, and salt to bowl; stir until well mixed. Transfer mixture to prepared loaf pan. Bake until instant-read thermometer inserted into center of loaf registers 160°F, about 1 hour 10 minutes. Let stand 10 minutes before slicing.

4 Meanwhile, to make sauce, whisk together broth, apple juice, and cornstarch in cup until smooth. Add to onion mixture in skillet; bring to boil. Reduce heat and simmer, stirring occasionally, until sauce begins to thicken, about 1 minute. Cut meatloaf into 12 slices. Serve with sauce.

Per serving (2 slices meatloaf with ¼ cup sauce): 281 Cal, 10 g Total Fat, 3 g Sat Fat, 0 g Trans Fat, 104 mg Chol, 534 mg Sod, 21 g Carb, 11 g Sugar, 2 g Fib, 26 g Prot, 52 mg Calc.

STORE AND SERVE LATER
Prepare the meatloaf and sauce through step 4, but do not slice. Transfer to an airtight container and let cool. Cover and refrigerate up to 4 days or freeze up to 3 months. To reheat, if frozen, thaw the meatloaf and sauce in the refrigerator overnight. Preheat the oven to 350°F. Cut the meatloaf into slices and arrange in a 9 x 13-inch baking dish, overlapping slices to fit. Top with sauce. Cover and bake until meatloaf is heated through and sauce is bubbly, about 25 minutes.

Lebanese Eggplant Stuffed with Beef, Feta, and Walnuts Serves 4

▲ 2   small (8-ounce) eggplants, halved lengthwise

1   teaspoon olive oil

▲ ½   pound lean ground beef (7% fat or less)

▲ 1   onion, finely chopped

▲ 1   tomato, chopped

⅓   cup whole wheat bread crumbs

¼   cup crumbled reduced-fat feta cheese

2   tablespoons walnuts, toasted and chopped

8   kalamata olives, pitted and chopped

▲ 1   large egg white, lightly beaten

¼   teaspoon salt

1   cup fat-free marinara sauce

1   Preheat oven to 400°F. Spray small shallow baking dish with nonstick spray.

2   Bring large pot of water to boil. Add eggplant; reduce heat and simmer, covered, until eggplant is just tender, about 5 minutes. Drain; let cool.

3   Meanwhile, heat oil in large nonstick skillet over medium-high heat. Add beef and onion and cook, stirring occasionally, until browned, about 5 minutes. Transfer to large bowl.

4   Carefully scoop out pulp from each eggplant half, leaving a ¼-inch thick shell. Coarsely chop pulp.

5   Add eggplant pulp to beef mixture in bowl. Stir in tomato, bread crumbs, cheese, walnuts, olives, egg white, and salt until well mixed. Spoon filling evenly into eggplant shells. Spoon marinara sauce into prepared baking dish; arrange eggplant on top of sauce. Bake, uncovered, until filling is hot and browned on top, about 25 minutes.

Per serving (½ stuffed eggplant with ¼ cup marinara sauce): 317 Cal, 13 g Total Fat, 4 g Sat Fat, 0 g Trans Fat, 107 mg Chol, 811 mg Sod, 24 g Carb, 7 g Sugar, 8 g Fib, 25 g Prot, 111 mg Calc.

STORE AND SERVE LATER

Prepare the eggplant through step 5, but do not bake. Cover and refrigerate up to 4 days or freeze up to 3 months. To reheat, if frozen, thaw the eggplant in the refrigerator overnight. Preheat the oven to 400°F. Uncover and bake until the filling is hot, about 25 minutes.

Pairs Well With: Orange and Fennel Salad, page 87

Southwestern Beef and Sweet Potato Shepherd's Pie Serves 6

▲ 2   **large sweet potatoes, peeled and cut into 1-inch cubes**

▲ 1   **(16-ounce) jar fat-free chipotle salsa**

1   **teaspoon unsalted butter, softened**

▲ 3/4   **pound lean ground beef (7% fat or less)**

▲ 2   **poblano chiles, chopped or 1 (4-ounce) can mild green chiles**

▲ 1   **(15 1/2-ounce) can black beans, rinsed and drained**

▲ 1   **cup frozen corn kernels, thawed**

1 Preheat oven to 375°F. Spray 1½-quart baking dish with nonstick spray.

2 To make potato topping, place potatoes in large pot with enough cold water to cover; bring to boil. Cook until potatoes are fork-tender, about 15 minutes. Drain and return to pot. Add ¼ cup salsa and butter; mash with potato masher until potatoes are smooth. Set aside.

3 Meanwhile, to make filling, spray large nonstick skillet with nonstick spray and set over medium-high heat. Add beef, breaking beef apart with back of spoon, and cook until browned, about 5 minutes. Add poblanos, beans, corn, and remaining salsa. Cook, stirring, until mixture comes to a boil and thickens slightly, about 8 minutes. Spoon filling into prepared baking dish.

4 Spread potato topping over beef mixture. Bake until topping is lightly browned and filling is bubbly along edges, 30 minutes. Let stand 5 minutes before serving.

Per serving (1 cup): 292 Cal, 6 g Total Fat, 2 g Sat Fat, 0 g Trans Fat, 52 mg Chol, 587 mg Sod, 35 g Carb, 6 g Sugar, 6 g Fib, 23 g Prot, 54 mg Calc.

STORE AND SERVE LATER

Omit step 1. Prepare the potato topping; transfer to an airtight container and let cool. Prepare the filling; transfer to a separate airtight container and let cool. Cover and refrigerate topping and filling up to 4 days. To reheat, preheat the oven to 375°F. Spray a 1½-quart baking dish with nonstick spray. Transfer the filling to the prepared dish. Top with the potato topping. Bake until heated through, about 30 minutes.

Beef and Spinach–Stuffed Lasagna Serves 6

▲ 6   whole wheat lasagna noodles

2   teaspoons olive oil

▲ ¹/₂   pound lean ground beef (7% or less fat)

▲ ¹/₂   pound cremini mushrooms, chopped

2   garlic cloves, minced

▲ 1   (5-ounce) container baby spinach

¹/₂   cup part-skim ricotta cheese

¹/₄   cup chopped fresh basil

3   tablespoons grated Parmesan cheese

1   (15 ¹/₂-ounce) jar fat-free marinara sauce

1 Cook lasagna noodles according to package directions. Drain, rinse noodles; drain again.

2 Heat oil in large nonstick skillet over medium-high heat. Add beef, mushrooms, and garlic. Cook, stirring occasionally, until mushrooms are tender, about 10 minutes. Add spinach and cook, stirring constantly, until spinach begins to wilt, about 2 minutes. Transfer beef mixture to bowl; let cool slightly. Add ricotta, basil, and 2 tablespoons Parmesan and stir until well mixed.

3 Preheat oven to 350°F. Spray 9 x 9-inch baking dish with cooking spray.

4 Spread ¹/₂ cup marinara sauce into prepared dish. Place cooked noodles on flat surface. Spread about ¹/₄ cup beef mixture over each noodle. Starting with a short-side, roll up, jelly-roll fashion. Place, seam side down, in baking dish. Pour remaining sauce over rolls. Loosely cover with foil and bake until hot and bubbly, about 30 minutes. Sprinkle with remaining 1 tablespoon Parmesan.

Per serving (1 roll with about ¹/₃ cup sauce): 253 Cal, 7 g Total Fat, 3 g Sat Fat, 0 g Trans Fat, 31 mg Chol, 407 mg Sod, 28 g Carb, 2 g Sugar, 6 g Fib, 18 g Prot, 162 mg Calc.

STORE AND SERVE LATER
Prepare the lasagna through step 4, but do not bake. Cover and refrigerate up to 4 days or freeze up to 3 months. To reheat, if frozen, thaw the lasagna in the refrigerator overnight. Preheat the oven to 350°F. Bake, covered, until heated through, about 30 minutes.

Beef and Spinach–Stuffed Lasagna and Arugula and Parmesan Salad, 87

Korean BBQ Pork Tenderloin with Kimchi Fried Rice Serves 4

2 tablespoons reduced-sodium soy sauce

1 tablespoon chili-garlic sauce

2 teaspoons hoisin sauce

▲ 1 (1-pound) lean pork tenderloin, trimmed

2 teaspoons canola oil

4 ounces prepared kimchi

▲ 1 (8.8-ounce) package cooked brown rice (about 1³/₄ cups)

1 Preheat oven to 425°F. Spray small roasting pan with nonstick spray.

2 Combine soy sauce, chili-garlic sauce, and hoisin sauce in shallow dish; add pork, turning to coat all sides.

3 Place pork in prepared pan and roast, turning occasionally, until instant-read thermometer inserted into center of pork registers 145°F for medium, about 15 minutes. Transfer pork to cutting board; let stand 10 minutes.

4 Meanwhile, to prepare rice, heat oil in large nonstick skillet over medium-high heat. Add kimchi and cook, stirring occasionally, until softened, about 8 minutes. Add rice and cook, stirring occasionally, until rice and kimchi just begin to brown, about 8 minutes.

5 Cut pork into 12 slices and serve with rice.

Per serving (3 slices pork with ²/₃ cup fried rice): 279 Cal, 7 g Total Fat, 1 g Sat Fat, 0 g Trans Fat, 62 mg Chol, 836 mg Sod, 21 g Carb, 1 g Sugar, 2 g Fib, 26 g Prot, 6 mg Calc.

STORE AND SERVE LATER

Omit step 1. Combine the pork, soy sauce, chili-garlic sauce, and hoisin sauce in a large zip-close plastic bag. Seal and refrigerate up to 2 days or freeze up to 3 months. Transfer the rice mixture to airtight container and let cool. Cover and refrigerate up to 4 days. If frozen, thaw the pork in the refrigerator overnight. To cook the pork, prepare as directed in steps 1 and 3. To reheat rice mixture, transfer to large microwavable dish, cover with wax paper, and microwave on High until heated through, 3–4 minutes.

Grilled Pork Tacos with Chipotle Vidalia Onions Serves 4

▲ 1 **(1-pound) lean pork tenderloin, trimmed**

¹/₂ **teaspoon salt**

2 **teaspoons olive oil**

▲ 2 **Vidalia or other sweet onions, thinly sliced**

▲ 1 **tomato, chopped**

2 **tablespoons minced chipotles en adobo**

³/₄ **teaspoon ground cumin**

¹/₄ **cup chopped fresh cilantro**

4 **(6-inch) multigrain tortillas, warmed**

¹/₄ **cup shredded Manchego cheese**

1 Spray nonstick ridged grill pan with nonstick spray and set over medium heat. Sprinkle pork with ¹/₄ teaspoon salt. Place pork in pan and grill, turning occasionally, until instant-read thermometer inserted into center of pork registers 145°F for medium, about 20 minutes. Transfer pork to cutting board; let stand 10 minutes. Slice pork into ¹/₄-inch-thick slices.

2 Meanwhile, heat oil in large nonstick skillet over medium heat. Add onions and cook, stirring occasionally, until softened, 5 minutes. Add tomato, chipotles, cumin, and remaining ¹/₄ teaspoon salt. Reduce heat to medium-low. Cover and cook, stirring occasionally, until onions are very soft and golden brown, about 25 minutes. Stir in cilantro.

3 Divide pork evenly among tortillas. Top evenly with onion mixture and sprinkle with cheese.

Per serving (1 taco): 353 Cal, 13 g Total Fat, 4 g Sat Fat, 0 g Trans Fat, 72 mg Chol, 887 mg Sod, 35 g Carb, 9 g Sugar, 16 g Fib, 38 g Prot, 195 mg Calc. PointsPlus value: 9.

9 PointsPlus value

STORE AND SERVE LATER

Transfer the pork slices and onion mixture to separate airtight containers and let cool. Cover and refrigerate up to 4 days or freeze up to 3 months. To reheat, if frozen, thaw the pork and the onion mixture in the refrigerator overnight. Transfer side by side to a large microwavable dish, cover with wax paper, and microwave on High until heated through, 5–6 minutes. Divide the pork evenly among 4 warmed (6-inch) multigrain tortillas. Top evenly with the onion mixture and with ¹/₄ cup shredded Manchego cheese.

Pairs Well With: Orzo with Corn and Bell Pepper, page 180

Spicy Korean Grilled Pork Bulgogi

Spicy Korean Grilled Pork Bulgogi Serves 4

1	**tablespoon grated peeled fresh ginger**
1	**tablespoon chili-garlic sauce**
3	**teaspoons packed brown sugar**
1	**teaspoon reduced-sodium soy sauce**
▲ 1	**(1-pound) lean pork tenderloin, trimmed**
▲ 2	**sweet onions (about 1 pound), cut crosswise into 1/2-inch slices**
1	**tablespoon rice vinegar**
1/2	**teaspoon Asian (dark) sesame oil**
1/4	**teaspoon salt**

1 Spray grill rack with nonstick spray. Preheat grill to medium-high or prepare medium-high fire.

2 Combine ginger, chili-garlic sauce, 2 teaspoons brown sugar, and soy sauce in shallow dish. Add pork, turning to coat all sides.

3 Place pork on grill rack and grill, turning occasionally, until pork is glazed and browned and instant-read thermometer inserted into center of pork registers 145°F, about 15 minutes. Transfer pork to cutting board; let stand 10 minutes.

4 Meanwhile, spray onion slices lightly on both sides with cooking spray. Place onions on grill rack and grill until browned and tender, 6–7 minutes on each side. Transfer to large bowl. Add vinegar, remaining 1 teaspoon brown sugar, sesame oil, and salt to bowl; toss to coat.

5 Cut pork into 12 slices and serve with onion mixture.

Per serving (3 slices pork with 1/2 cup onion mixture): 199 Cal, 4 g Total Fat, 1 g Sat Fat, 0 g Trans Fat, 62 mg Chol, 303 mg Sod, 17 g Carb, 12 g Sugar, 2 g Fib, 24 g Prot, 42 mg Calc.

STORE AND SERVE LATER
Omit step 1. Combine the pork, ginger, chili-garlic sauce, brown sugar, and soy sauce in a large zip-close plastic bag. Seal and refrigerate up to 2 days or freeze up to 3 months. If frozen, thaw the pork in the refrigerator overnight. To cook the pork, prepare as directed in steps 1 and 3. Prepare the onions as directed in step 4.

Pairs Well With: Brown Rice, Squash, and Scallion Stir-Fry, page 180

Coconut-Curry Braised Pork with Apples Serves 4

▲ 4   (¹/₄-pound) boneless lean center-cut pork loin chops, trimmed

¹/₂   teaspoon salt

2   teaspoons canola oil

▲ 1   onion, thinly sliced

▲ 1   cup reduced-sodium chicken broth

▲ 2   small Granny Smith apples, cored and cut into ¹/₄-inch thick slices

2   teaspoons grated peeled fresh ginger

2   garlic cloves, minced

¹/₂   cup light (reduced-fat) coconut milk

2   teaspoons Thai red curry paste

2   teaspoons packed brown sugar

2   tablespoons chopped fresh cilantro

1 Sprinkle pork with ¹/₄ teaspoon salt. Heat oil in large nonstick skillet over medium-high heat. Add pork and cook, turning occasionally, until browned, about 6 minutes. Transfer to plate.

2 Add onion and ¹/₄ cup broth to skillet; bring to boil. Reduce heat and simmer, covered, stirring occasionally, until onion is softened, about 5 minutes. Add apples, ginger, and garlic, and cook, stirring often, until apple is tender, about 5 minutes. Add remaining ³/₄ cup broth, coconut milk, curry paste, and sugar; bring to boil, stirring until sauce is thickened slightly, about 5 minutes. Return pork chops and any accumulated juices to skillet. Reduce heat and simmer, uncovered, until chops are heated through, 3–4 minutes. Remove from heat; stir in cilantro.

Per serving (1 pork chop with ¹/₂ cup sauce): 258 Cal, 11 g Total Fat, 2 g Sat Fat, 0 g Trans Fat, 66 mg Chol, 451 mg Sod, 19 g Carb, 12 g Sugar, 3 g Fib, 23 g Prot, 43 mg Calc.

STORE AND SERVE LATER
Transfer the pork and sauce to an airtight container and let cool. Cover and refrigerate up to 4 days or freeze up to 3 months. If frozen, thaw the pork and sauce in the refrigerator overnight. Transfer to a large microwavable dish, cover with wax paper, and microwave on High until heated through, 5–6 minutes.

Pork, Potato, and Green Chile Stew Serves 4

2 teaspoons olive oil

▲ 1 (1-pound) lean pork tenderloin, trimmed and cut into ¾-inch cubes

▲ 1 onion, chopped

2 garlic cloves, minced

▲ 2 cups reduced-sodium chicken broth

▲ 1 cup fat-free green salsa

1 teaspoon ground cumin

¼ teaspoon salt

▲ 2 russet potatoes, peeled and cubed

▲ 1 zucchini, diced

½ cup chopped fresh cilantro

1 Heat oil in large saucepan over medium-high heat. Add pork and cook, stirring frequently, until browned, about 5 minutes. Transfer to plate.

2 Add onion and garlic to saucepan and cook, stirring frequently, until onion is softened, about 5 minutes. Add broth, salsa, cumin, and salt; bring to boil. Add potatoes and zucchini; return to boil. Reduce heat and simmer, uncovered, until vegetables are tender, about 20 minutes.

3 Return pork and any accumulated juices to saucepan; cook, stirring occasionally, until heated through, 2–3 minutes. Remove from heat; stir in cilantro.

Per serving (1⅔ cups): 254 Cal, 6 g Total Fat, 2 g Sat Fat, 0 g Trans Fat, 62 mg Chol, 467 mg Sod, 24 g Carb, 7 g Sugar, 3 g Fib, 28 g Prot, 44 mg Calc.

STORE AND SERVE LATER
Transfer the stew to an airtight container and let cool. Cover and refrigerate up to 4 days. To reheat, transfer to a medium saucepan. Cover and cook over medium heat, stirring occasionally, until heated through, 8–10 minutes.

Pairs Well With: Lemony Spinach and Avocado Salad, page 86

Veggie Sides to Serve 4

Buttered Broccoli with Lemon and Parmesan

Place **4 cups broccoli florets** in medium microwave-safe dish; cover with wax paper and microwave on High until crisp-tender, about 3 minutes. Drain and transfer to serving bowl. Add **2 teaspoons butter, grated zest and juice of ½ lemon,** and **¼ teaspoon salt** and toss to coat. Sprinkle with **1 tablespoon grated Parmesan.**

Roasted Zucchini with Yogurt and Mint

Preheat oven to 425°F. Cut **4 small zucchini lengthwise into quarters;** place in medium baking pan. Add **2 teaspoons olive oil, ¼ teaspoon salt,** and **⅛ teaspoon black pepper** and toss to coat. Bake, turning once, until zucchini are tender, 20–25 minutes. Transfer to serving platter; dollop with **¼ cup plain low-fat Greek yogurt.** Sprinkle with **2 tablespoons chopped fresh mint.**

Asparagus with Roasted Red Peppers and Capers

Heat **1 tablespoon olive oil** in large skillet over medium-high heat. Add **1 pound asparagus,** cut into 2-inch pieces, and cook, stirring often, until crisp-tender, about 5 minutes. Add **½ cup thinly sliced roasted red peppers (not in oil), 1 tablespoon capers, drained, 1 garlic clove, minced,** and **⅛ teaspoon black pepper.** Cook, stirring constantly, until heated through, about 1 minute. Stir in **1 tablespoon minced fresh flat-leaf parsley.**

Minted Green Beans with Pine Nuts

Bring large saucepan of water to boil. Add **1 pound trimmed green beans** and cook until crisp-tender, about 5 minutes. Drain. Transfer to serving bowl; add **2 tablespoons chopped fresh mint, 2 tablespoons toasted pine nuts, 2 teaspoons olive oil, grated zest and juice from 1 lemon,** ¼ **teaspoon salt,** and ⅛ **teaspoon black pepper** and toss to coat.

Buttery Crumb-Topped Cauliflower

Bring medium saucepan of water to boil; add **4 cups cauliflower florets** and cook until tender, about 5 minutes. Drain. Heat **2 teaspoons butter** in large nonstick skillet over medium heat; add ⅓ **cup panko bread crumbs** and cook, stirring, until crumbs are toasted, about 3 minutes. Transfer to bowl. Wipe out skillet and add **2 teaspoons olive oil.** Set over medium-high heat. Add cauliflower, **1 garlic clove, minced,** ¼ **teaspoon salt,** and ⅛ **teaspoon red pepper flakes;** cook, stirring often, until cauliflower is lightly browned, 5 minutes. Add crumbs and toss to combine.

Roasted Brussels Sprouts with Walnuts and Lemon

Preheat oven to 425°F. Cut **1 pound Brussels sprouts** lengthwise into quarters; place in medium baking pan. Add **2 teaspoons olive oil,** ¼ **teaspoon salt,** and ⅛ **teaspoon black pepper** and toss to coat. Bake, stirring once, until Brussels sprouts are tender, 20–25 minutes. Transfer to serving dish; add **2 tablespoons chopped walnuts, 2 teaspoons grated lemon zest,** and **1 tablespoon lemon juice.** Toss to coat.

Rosemary Parmesan Oven Fries

Preheat oven to 425°F. Cut **1 pound baking potatoes** into ½-inch sticks; place on medium baking pan. Add **2 teaspoons olive oil,** ¼ **teaspoon salt,** and ⅛ **teaspoon black pepper** and toss to coat. Bake, turning once, until potatoes are tender and browned, about 30 minutes. Transfer potatoes to serving platter; sprinkle with **2 tablespoons grated Parmesan cheese, 1 garlic clove, minced,** and **1 teaspoon minced fresh rosemary** and toss to coat.

Maple-Orange Mashed Sweet Potatoes

Pierce **2 large sweet potatoes** (about 1½ pounds) in several places with fork. Place in microwave-safe dish and cook on High until tender, 10–12 minutes. Let cool slightly. Cut each potato in half; scoop out flesh and place in medium bowl. Add **1 tablespoon maple syrup, 2 teaspoons butter, 1 teaspoon grated orange zest,** and ¼ **teaspoon salt** and mash with potato masher.

Garlicky Pork and Bean Stew with Parmesan Crisps Serves 8

½ cup shredded Parmesan cheese

▲ 4 (4-ounce) boneless lean center-cut pork chops, trimmed and cut into ¾-inch pieces

½ teaspoon salt

2 teaspoons olive oil

▲ 1½ pounds Swiss chard, stems and leaves coarsely chopped

3 garlic cloves, minced

▲ 1 (15 ½-ounce) can cannellini beans, rinsed and drained

▲ 1 (14 ½-ounce) can diced tomatoes

▲ 1 cup reduced-sodium chicken broth

1 Preheat oven to 400°F. Line large baking sheet with parchment paper. Drop cheese by tablespoonfuls onto baking sheet, about 2 inches apart, making total of 8 mounds. Spread each mound into 2-inch round. Bake until golden, 5–7 minutes. Let crisps cool on baking sheet 1 minute. Using wide spatula, transfer crisps to wire rack to cool completely.

2 Meanwhile, sprinkle pork with salt. Heat 1 teaspoon oil in Dutch oven over medium-high heat. Add pork and cook, stirring frequently, until browned, about 5 minutes. Transfer to plate.

3 Add remaining 1 teaspoon oil to Dutch oven. Reduce heat to medium. Add Swiss chard, in batches if necessary, and garlic and cook, stirring constantly, until chard is wilted, about 3 minutes. Add beans, tomatoes, and broth; bring to boil. Reduce heat and simmer, covered, stirring occasionally, until Swiss chard is tender, about 20 minutes. Return pork and any accumulated juices to Dutch oven; cook until heated through, about 2 minutes. Serve with cheese crisps.

Per serving (1¼ cups stew and 1 crisp): 184 Cal, 6 g Total Fat, 2 g Sat Fat, 0 g Trans Fat, 37 mg Chol, 709 mg Sod, 15 g Carb, 4 g Sugar, 4 g Fib, 18 g Prot, 152 mg Calc.

4 PointsPlus value

STORE AND SERVE LATER
Place the cooled Parmesan crisps in an airtight container, layering them between sheets of wax paper. Store at room temperature up to 3 days. Transfer the stew to an airtight container and let cool. Cover and refrigerate up to 4 days or freeze up to 3 months. To reheat, if frozen, thaw the stew in the refrigerator overnight. Transfer to a medium saucepan. Cover and cook over medium heat, stirring occasionally, until heated through, 8–10 minutes.

North African Lamb Stew with Dates and Almonds

Serves 4

2 teaspoons canola oil

1 pound boneless lean lamb shoulder, trimmed and cut into 1-inch cubes

▲ 1 red onion, thinly sliced

2 garlic cloves, minced

1 tablespoon fennel seeds, crushed

1 tablespoon grated peeled fresh ginger

1½ teaspoons ground coriander

1 teaspoon ground cinnamon

▲ 2½ cups reduced-sodium beef broth

½ teaspoon salt

▲ 2 sweet potatoes, peeled and cut into ¾-inch pieces

¼ cup pitted dates, halved lengthwise

¼ cup dried apricots, cut into thin strips

¼ cup chopped fresh cilantro

2 tablespoons sliced almonds, toasted

1 Heat oil in large saucepan over medium-high heat. Add lamb and cook, stirring often, until browned, about 3 minutes. Transfer to plate. Add onion and cook, stirring occasionally, until softened, 3 minutes. Add garlic, fennel, ginger, coriander, and cinnamon and cook, stirring constantly, until fragrant, 30 seconds.

2 Return lamb and any accumulated juices to saucepan. Add broth and salt; bring to boil. Reduce heat and simmer, covered, until lamb is almost tender, about 30 minutes. Add sweet potatoes; reduce heat and simmer, covered, until potatoes are tender, about 20 minutes. Stir in dates and apricots and cook until heated through, 2 minutes.

3 Ladle stew evenly into 4 bowls and sprinkle evenly with cilantro and almonds.

Per serving (1¼ cups): 338 Cal, 13 g Total Fat, 3 g Sat Fat, 0 g Trans Fat, 68 mg Chol, 426 mg Sod, 30 g Carb, 17 g Sugar, 5 g Fib, 26 g Prot, 82 mg Calc.

9 PointsPlus® value

STORE AND SERVE LATER

Prepare the stew through step 2. Transfer to an airtight container and let cool. Cover and refrigerate up to 4 days or freeze up to 3 months. To reheat, if frozen, thaw the stew in the refrigerator overnight. Transfer to a medium saucepan. Cover and cook over medium heat, stirring occasionally, until heated through 8–10 minutes. Ladle the stew evenly into 4 bowls; sprinkle evenly with ¼ cup chopped fresh cilantro and 2 tablespoons toasted sliced almonds.

Pairs Well With: **Asparagus with Roasted Red Peppers and Capers, page 36**

Spicy Sweet Potato–Corn Chowder with Ham Serves 6

2 teaspoons olive oil

▲ 1 onion, finely chopped

▲ 2 stalks celery, chopped

2 garlic cloves, minced

2 teaspoons all-purpose flour

¼ teaspoon cayenne

▲ 1 (32-ounce) carton reduced-sodium chicken broth

▲ 1 large sweet potato, peeled and cut into ½-inch cubes

1 chipotle en adobo, minced

¼ teaspoon salt

▲ 2 cups fresh or frozen corn kernels

▲ 1 (6-ounce) reduced-sodium lean ham steak, trimmed and cut into ½-inch cubes

▲ ½ cup fat-free half-and-half

2 tablespoons minced fresh chives

1 Heat oil in large saucepan over medium-high heat. Add onion, celery, and garlic and cook, stirring frequently, until vegetables are softened, about 5 minutes. Stir in flour and cayenne and cook, stirring constantly, 1 minute.

2 Add broth, sweet potato, chipotle, and salt; bring to boil. Reduce heat, cover, and simmer until potato is tender, about 10 minutes. Stir in corn, ham, and half-and-half and cook until heated through, 2–3 minutes longer.

3 Ladle soup evenly into 6 bowls and sprinkle with chives.

Per serving (generous 1 cup): 185 Cal, 5 g Total Fat, 1 g Sat Fat, 0 g Trans Fat, 15 mg Chol, 472 mg Sod, 25 g Carb, 5 g Sugar, 2 g Fib, 12 g Prot, 63 mg Calc. PointsPlus value: 5.

STORE AND SERVE LATER

Transfer the stew to an airtight container and let cool. Cover and refrigerate up to 4 days or freeze up to 3 months. To reheat, if frozen, thaw the stew in the refrigerator overnight. Transfer to a medium saucepan. Cover and cook over medium heat, stirring occasionally, until heated through, 8–10 minutes. Ladle the soup evenly into 4 bowls and sprinkle evenly with 2 tablespoons minced fresh chives.

Pairs Well With: Cranberry-Carrot Slaw, page 87

**Spicy Sweet Potato–Corn
Chowder with Ham**

Kofta with Couscous Serves 4

1	**pound lean ground lamb**
1	**shallot, minced**
1	**garlic clove, minced**
1	**teaspoon ground cumin**
1/2	**teaspoon ground allspice**
1/2	**teaspoon salt**
2	**teaspoons olive oil**
▲ 1	**large sweet onion, finely chopped**
▲ 1	**jalapeño pepper, seeded and minced**
1	**tablespoon minced peeled fresh ginger**
▲ 2	**cups reduced-sodium chicken broth**
1	**lemon, cut into 6 wedges and seeded**
▲ 1	**cup whole wheat couscous**
1/4	**cup chopped fresh mint**

1 Mix together lamb, shallot, garlic, cumin, allspice, and salt in large bowl until thoroughly combined. With damp hands, shape mixture into 16 (1-inch) balls.

2 Heat oil in large skillet over medium-high heat. Add meatballs and cook, turning often, until browned on all sides, about 5 minutes. Add onion, jalapeno, and ginger; cook, stirring occasionally, until onion begins to soften, 2–3 minutes.

3 Add broth and lemon wedges. Reduce heat, cover, and simmer, stirring gently once or twice, until meatballs are cooked through, about 10 minutes. Remove and discard lemon wedges.

4 Meanwhile, prepare couscous according to package directions. Divide couscous evenly among 4 bowls; top evenly with meatball mixture. Sprinkle with mint.

Per serving (4 meatballs with 3/4 cup broth mixture and 1/2 cup couscous): 335 Cal, 10 g Total Fat, 3 g Sat Fat, 0 g Trans Fat, 64 mg Chol, 395 mg Sod, 36 g Carb, 5 g Sugar, 6 g Fib, 28 g Prot, 75 mg Calc.

9 PointsPlus® value

STORE AND SERVE LATER
Prepare meatballs through step 2. Transfer to an airtight container and let cool. Cover and refrigerate up to 4 days or freeze up to 3 months. To reheat, if frozen, thaw the meatballs in the refrigerator overnight. Transfer meatballs to a medium saucepan. Add 2 cups reduced-sodium chicken broth and 1 lemon, cut into 6 wedges and seeded. Bring to a boil; reduce heat, cover, and simmer, stirring gently once or twice, until meatballs are cooked through, about 10 minutes. Remove and discard lemon wedges. Meanwhile, prepare 1 cup whole wheat couscous according to package directions. Divide couscous evenly among 4 serving bowls; top evenly with meatball mixture. Sprinkle evenly with 1/4 cup chopped fresh mint.

Chicken and Quinoa Salad with Dried Fruit and Pine Nuts Serves 4

▲ 1/2 cup red or white quinoa

1 cup water

▲ 1/2 cup thawed frozen green peas

▲ 4 (5-ounce) skinless, boneless chicken breasts

1/2 teaspoon ground fennel seeds

1/4 teaspoon salt

1/4 cup dried apricots, thinly sliced

1/4 cup golden raisins

▲ 2 scallions, thinly sliced

2 tablespoons orange juice

1 tablespoon seasoned rice vinegar

2 teaspoons extra-virgin olive oil

1 tablespoon toasted pine nuts

1 Combine quinoa and water in small saucepan; bring to boil. Reduce heat; cover and simmer until liquid is absorbed and quinoa is tender, about 12 minutes, adding peas during last 2 minutes of cooking time. Drain quinoa mixture in fine-mesh strainer; rinse under cold running water and drain again. Transfer to large bowl.

2 Meanwhile, sprinkle chicken with fennel seeds and salt. Spray large nonstick ridged grill pan with nonstick spray and set over medium-high heat. Add chicken and cook, turning occasionally, until well browned and cooked through, about 8 minutes. Transfer chicken to cutting board; let stand 5 minutes. Cut chicken into thin slices.

3 Add apricots, raisins, scallions, orange juice, vinegar, and oil to quinoa in bowl; add chicken and toss to combine. Just before serving, sprinkle with pine nuts.

Per serving (1 cup): 342 Cal, 9 g Total Fat, 2 g Sat Fat, 0 g Trans Fat, 78 mg Chol, 310 mg Sod, 32 g Carb, 14 g Sugar, 4 g Fib, 34 g Prot, 49 mg Calc.

9 PointsPlus© value

STORE AND SERVE LATER

Prepare the salad, omitting the pine nuts. Transfer to an airtight container and refrigerate up to 2 days. Sprinkle with 1 tablespoon toasted pine nuts just before serving.

Finish With: Maple-Mint Fruit Compote, page 130

Yucatan Chicken with Black Beans and Rice Serves 4

- ▲ 1 pound skinless, boneless chicken breasts, cut into 1-inch pieces
- 2 tablespoons achiote paste or 1 tablespoon smoked paprika
- 2 ounces cured chorizo sausage, diced
- ▲ 1 onion, chopped
- 2 garlic cloves, minced
- ▲ 1½ cups reduced-sodium chicken broth
- ▲ ½ cup brown rice
- ▲ 1 (15 ½-ounce) can black beans, rinsed and drained
- ▲ ½ cup fat-free habanero salsa
- 2 tablespoons chopped fresh cilantro
- 4 lime wedges

1 Combine chicken and 1 tablespoon achiote paste in medium bowl; toss to coat.

2 Spray large deep nonstick skillet with nonstick spray and set over medium-high heat. Add chicken and cook, turning occasionally, until browned, about 5 minutes. Transfer chicken to plate.

3 Add chorizo to skillet and cook, stirring occasionally, until browned, about 3 minutes. Add onion and garlic, spraying skillet with additional nonstick spray if necessary, and cook, stirring occasionally, until onion is softened, about 5 minutes. Add broth, rice, and remaining 1 tablespoon achiote paste; bring to boil. Reduce heat and simmer, covered, until liquid is absorbed and rice is tender, 35–40 minutes. Return chicken to skillet.

4 Add beans and salsa; cook, stirring occasionally, until heated through, about 3 minutes. Remove from heat and stir in cilantro. Serve with lime wedges.

Per serving (1¼ cups): 405 Cal, 10 g Total Fat, 3 g Sat Fat, 0 g Trans Fat, 75 mg Chol, 715 mg Sod, 42 g Carb, 4 g Sugar, 7 g Fib, 36 g Prot, 76 mg Calc.

STORE AND SERVE LATER

Prepare chicken mixture through step 3. Transfer to an airtight container and let cool. Cover and refrigerate up to 4 days. To reheat, transfer to a large deep nonstick skillet. Add 1 (15½-ounce) can black beans, rinsed and drained, and ½ cup fat-free habanero salsa; cook, stirring occasionally, until heated through, 8–10 minutes. Remove from heat and stir in 2 tablespoons chopped fresh cilantro. Serve with lime wedges.

Rosemary Roasted Chicken and Vegetables with Bacon Serves 4

▲ 2 **russet potatoes, peeled and cut into 1-inch cubes**

▲ 2 **red bell peppers, sliced**

▲ 1 **large leek, cleaned and thinly sliced (white and light green parts only)**

2 **teaspoons olive oil**

1 **tablespoon chopped fresh rosemary**

3/4 **teaspoon salt**

▲ 1 **pound skinless, boneless chicken breasts, cut into 1-inch pieces**

2 **strips bacon, coarsely chopped**

1 Preheat oven to 425°F.

2 Combine potatoes, bell peppers, leek, oil, 2 teaspoons rosemary, and 1/2 teaspoon salt in large shallow roasting pan; toss to coat. Roast about 20 minutes.

3 Meanwhile sprinkle chicken with remaining 1 teaspoon rosemary and remaining 1/4 teaspoon salt. Spray large nonstick skillet with nonstick spray and set over medium-high heat. Add chicken and cook, turning occasionally, until browned, about 5 minutes.

4 Place chicken on top of vegetables and roast, stirring occasionally, until chicken is cooked through and vegetables are tender, about 25 minutes longer.

5 Meanwhile, cook bacon in medium skillet over medium heat, stirring occasionally, until crisp and browned, about 5 minutes. Transfer to paper towels to drain. Sprinkle bacon over chicken and vegetables.

Per serving (about 1 1/4 cups chicken and vegetables): 267 Cal, 7 g Total Fat, 2 g Sat Fat, 0 g Trans Fat, 67 mg Chol, 594 mg Sod, 24 g Carb, 4 g Sugar, 3 g Fib, 27 g Prot, 37 mg Calc.

7 PointsPlus® value

STORE AND SERVE LATER

Prepare the chicken and vegetables through step 4. Transfer to an airtight container and let cool. Cover and refrigerate up to 4 days. To reheat, transfer to microwavable dish, cover with wax paper, and microwave on High until heated through 4–5 minutes. Prepare bacon as directed in step 5. Sprinkle over chicken and vegetables just before serving.

Pairs Well With: Tomato-Goat Cheese Salad with Balsamic Dressing, page 87

**Braised Lemon Chicken
with Moroccan Spices**

Braised Lemon Chicken with Moroccan Spices Serves 4

2	**teaspoons olive oil**
4	**skinless whole chicken legs (about 2 pounds)**
▲ **1**	**onion, thinly sliced**
1	**tablespoon minced peeled fresh ginger**
1	**teaspoon ground cumin**
1/2	**teaspoon ground cinnamon**
1/2	**teaspoon ground coriander**
1/4	**teaspoon salt**
▲ **3**	**carrots, thinly sliced**
▲ **1 1/2**	**cups reduced-sodium chicken broth**
	Grated zest and juice of 1 lemon
▲ **1**	**cup frozen green peas**
1	**tablespoon fresh mint leaves**

1 Heat 1 teaspoon oil in large deep nonstick skillet over medium-high heat. Add chicken and cook, turning occasionally, until browned, about 8 minutes. Transfer chicken to plate.

2 Add remaining 1 teaspoon oil to skillet and reduce heat to medium. Add onion and ginger; cook, stirring occasionally, until onion is softened, about 5 minutes. Stir in cumin, cinnamon, coriander, and salt. Cook, stirring constantly, until fragrant, 30 seconds.

3 Return chicken to skillet; add carrots, broth, and lemon zest and juice. Bring to boil. Reduce heat and simmer, covered, until chicken is cooked through, about 15 minutes.

4 Stir in peas; cook until heated through, about 3 minutes. Remove from heat and top with mint.

Per serving (1 whole chicken leg with 1/2 cup vegetables and sauce): 256 Cal, 8 g Total Fat, 2 g Sat Fat, 0 g Trans Fat, 98 mg Chol, 347 mg Sod, 16 g Carb, 7 g Sugar, 5 g Fib, 31 g Prot, 66 mg Calc.

STORE AND SERVE LATER

Prepare the chicken mixture through step 3. Transfer to an airtight container and let cool. Cover and refrigerate up to 4 days. To reheat, transfer to a large deep nonstick skillet. Cover and cook over medium heat, stirring occasionally, until heated through, 8–10 minutes. Stir in 1 cup frozen green peas and cook until heated through, about 3 minutes. Remove from heat and stir in 1 tablespoon chopped fresh mint.

Pairs Well With: Couscous-Carrot Pilaf, page 181

Chicken, Sausage, and White Bean Casserole Serves 4

4	(1/4-pound) skinless boneless chicken thighs, trimmed
3	ounces turkey kielbasa, thinly sliced
▲ 1	onion, chopped
▲ 2	carrots, sliced
▲ 1	celery stalk, chopped
3	garlic cloves, minced
▲ 1	(15 1/2-ounce) can no-salt-added small white beans, rinsed and drained
▲ 1	(14 1/2-ounce) can no-salt-added diced tomatoes
▲ 1	cup reduced-sodium chicken broth
1/2	cup dry white wine
1/2	teaspoon dried thyme
1/2	cup fresh whole wheat bread crumbs
1	tablespoon chopped fresh parsley
	Grated zest of 1 lemon

1 Preheat oven to 350°F.

2 Spray Dutch oven with nonstick spray and set over medium-high heat. Add chicken and cook, turning occasionally, until browned, about 5 minutes. Transfer chicken to plate.

3 Add kielbasa to Dutch oven and cook, turning occasionally, until browned, 2–3 minutes. Add onion, carrots, celery, and 2 garlic cloves; cook, stirring frequently, until softened, about 5 minutes. Add beans, tomatoes, broth, wine, and thyme; bring to simmer.

4 Remove Dutch oven from heat; add chicken and any accumulated juices, nestling chicken among vegetables. Cover and bake until chicken is cooked through and sauce begins to thicken slightly, about 25 minutes.

5 Stir together bread crumbs, parsley, lemon zest, and remaining 1 garlic clove in small bowl. Remove Dutch oven from oven and uncover. Sprinkle with crumb mixture and lightly spray crumb mixture with nonstick spray. Bake, uncovered, until edges are bubbly and topping is browned, about 10 minutes.

Per serving (1 chicken thigh with about 3/4 cup vegetables and sauce): 389 Cal, 11 g Total Fat, 3 g Sat Fat, 0 g Trans Fat, 89 mg Chol, 349 mg Sod, 33 g Carb, 7 g Sugar, 9 g Fib, 32 g Prot, 122 mg Calc.

STORE AND SERVE LATER
Prepare the chicken mixture through step 4. Transfer to an airtight container and let cool. Cover and refrigerate up to 4 days or freeze for up to 4 months. To reheat, if frozen, thaw in the refrigerator overnight. Preheat oven to 350°F. Transfer the chicken mixture to a large baking dish. Prepare the crumb mixture as directed in step 5. Sprinkle over chicken mixture and bake, uncovered, until heated through, 25 minutes.

Chicken Vindaloo Serves 4

4 (¼-pound) skinless chicken drumsticks

2 teaspoons canola oil

▲ 2 onions, sliced

3 garlic cloves, minced

¾ cup water

2 teaspoons curry powder

1 teaspoon mustard seeds

1 teaspoon garam masala

½ teaspoon salt

¼ teaspoon red pepper flakes

▲ 2 tomatoes, chopped

2 tablespoons apple cider vinegar

1 teaspoon packed brown sugar

¼ cup chopped fresh cilantro

1 Spray large deep nonstick skillet with nonstick spray and set over medium-high heat. Add chicken and cook, turning occasionally, until browned, about 8 minutes. Transfer to plate.

2 Add oil to skillet. Add onions, garlic, and ¼ cup of water. Reduce heat to medium and cook, stirring occasionally, until onions are tender, 8 minutes. Add curry powder, mustard seeds, garam masala, salt, and red pepper flakes; cook, stirring constantly until fragrant, 30 seconds. Add tomatoes and cook, stirring occasionally, until softened, about 5 minutes. Add vinegar, brown sugar, and remaining ½ cup water; bring to boil.

3 Return chicken to skillet. Reduce heat, cover, and simmer until chicken is fork-tender, about 20 minutes.

4 Remove from heat and stir in cilantro.

Per serving (1 chicken drumstick and ½ cup sauce): 148 Cal, 5 g Total Fat, 1 g Sat Fat, 0 g Trans Fat, 49 mg Chol, 355 mg Sod, 12 g Carb, 7 g Sugar, 3 g Fib, 15 g Prot, 48 mg Calc.

STORE AND SERVE LATER

Prepare the chicken through step 3. Transfer to an airtight container and let cool. Cover and refrigerate up to 4 days or freeze for up to 4 months. To reheat, if frozen, thaw in the refrigerator overnight. Transfer to microwavable dish, cover with wax paper, and microwave on High until heated through 4–5 minutes. Stir in ¼ cup chopped fresh cilantro.

Pairs Well With: Minted Green Beans with Pine Nuts, page 37

Fiery Chili Chicken Legs Serves 4

4   **skinless whole chicken legs (about 2 pounds)**

1/2   **teaspoon ground cumin**

1/2   **teaspoon salt**

2   **teaspoons canola oil**

▲ 2   **red bell peppers, cut into 1-inch pieces**

▲ 1   **onion, sliced**

2   **garlic cloves, minced**

▲ 3/4   **cup reduced-sodium chicken broth**

2   **tablespoons chili-garlic sauce**

1   **tablespoon hoisin sauce**

2   **tablespoons chopped fresh cilantro**

2   **tablespoons chopped dry-roasted unsalted cashews**

1   Sprinkle chicken with cumin and salt. Heat 1 teaspoon oil in large nonstick skillet over medium-high heat. Add chicken and cook, turning occasionally, until browned, about 8 minutes. Transfer chicken to plate.

2   Add remaining 1 teaspoon oil to skillet. Add bell peppers, onion, and garlic; cook, stirring occasionally, until vegetables are slightly softened, about 5 minutes.

3   Return chicken and any accumulated juices to skillet. Add broth, chili-garlic sauce, and hoisin sauce; bring to boil. Reduce heat and simmer, covered, until chicken is cooked through and vegetables are tender, about 25 minutes.

4   Remove from heat and stir in cilantro; sprinkle with cashews.

Per serving (1 chicken leg with 1/3 cup pepper mixture):
261 Cal, 12 g Total Fat, 3 g Sat Fat, 0 g Trans Fat, 83 mg Chol, 578 mg Sod, 10 g Carb, 5 g Sugar, 2 g Fib, 27 g Prot, 29 mg Calc.

6 PointsPlus® value

STORE AND SERVE LATER

Prepare the chicken mixture through step 3. Transfer to an airtight container and let cool. Cover and refrigerate up to 4 days. To reheat, transfer to a large deep nonstick skillet. Cover and cook over medium heat, stirring occasionally, until heated through, 8–10 minutes. Remove from heat and stir in 2 tablespoons chopped fresh cilantro. Sprinkle with 2 tablespoons chopped dry-roasted unsalted cashews.

Fiery Chili Chicken Legs and
Orange and Fennel Salad, 87

Chicken-Mushroom Enchiladas with Tomatillo Sauce Serves 5

2 teaspoons olive oil

▲ 1 (10-ounce) package white mushrooms, sliced

▲ 1 (5-ounce) package baby spinach

2 garlic cloves, minced

1/2 teaspoon salt

▲ 2 cups cooked shredded skinless chicken breast

1 (28-ounce) can tomatillos, drained

1 cup chopped fresh cilantro

▲ 1/2 cup reduced-sodium chicken broth

▲ 1 jalapeño pepper, seeded and coarsely chopped

10 (6-inch) corn tortillas, warmed

3/4 cup shredded reduced-fat Monterey Jack cheese

1 Preheat oven to 375°F. Spray 9 x 13-inch baking dish with nonstick spray.

2 Heat oil in large nonstick skillet over medium-high heat. Add mushrooms and cook, stirring occasionally, until mushrooms are browned, about 8 minutes. Add spinach, garlic, and salt; cook, stirring, until spinach is wilted and any liquid is evaporated, about 3 minutes. Remove from heat; stir in chicken.

3 Meanwhile, puree tomatillos, cilantro, broth, and jalapeño in food processor. Spread about 1/2 cup tomatillo mixture into prepared baking dish. Place tortilla on work surface and top with about 1/4 cup of mushroom mixture. Fold two opposite sides of tortilla over to enclose filling. Place enchilada, seam side down, in baking dish. Repeat with remaining tortillas and mushroom mixture, making a total of 10 enchiladas. Pour remaining tomatillo mixture over enchiladas and sprinkle with cheese.

4 Spray sheet of foil with nonstick spray; cover baking dish with foil, coated side down, and bake 20 minutes. Remove foil and continue to bake until edges of enchiladas begin to brown and cheese is melted, about 10 minutes longer. Let stand 10 minutes before serving.

Per serving (2 enchiladas): 384 Cal, 11 g Total Fat, 3 g Sat Fat, 0 g Trans Fat, 57 mg Chol, 538 mg Sod, 43 g Carb, 5 g Sugar, 6 g Fib, 27 g Prot, 275 mg Calc.

STORE AND SERVE LATER
Prepare the enchiladas through step 3, but do not bake. Cover and refrigerate up to 4 days or freeze up to 4 months. If frozen, thaw the enchiladas in the refrigerator overnight. To reheat, preheat the oven to 375°F and proceed with step 4.

Meatless Moussaka Serves 6

▲ 1 large eggplant (1½ pounds), cut crosswise into 12 (½-inch) rounds

2 teaspoons olive oil

▲ 1 onion, finely chopped

3 garlic cloves, minced

1 (12-ounce) tube refrigerated TVP (textured vegetable protein)

▲ 1 (14½-ounce) can diced tomatoes

½ cup dry red wine

1 tablespoon chopped fresh oregano or 1½ teaspoons dried

1 teaspoon ground cinnamon

½ teaspoon ground allspice

½ teaspoon salt

▲ 1¾ cups fat-free milk

3 tablespoons all-purpose flour

▲ 1 large egg

⅛ teaspoon ground nutmeg

½ cup shredded Parmesan cheese

1 Spray broiler rack with nonstick spray; preheat broiler. Place eggplant rounds on broiler rack; lightly spray both sides of each round with olive oil nonstick spray. Arrange eggplant in single layer and broil 5 inches from heat, turning once, until lightly browned, about 10 minutes. Preheat oven to 375°F.

2 Meanwhile, heat oil in large nonstick skillet over medium-high heat. Add onion and garlic; cook, stirring occasionally, until soft, 6 minutes. Add TVP and cook, breaking apart with spoon until browned, 5 minutes. Stir in tomatoes, wine, oregano, cinnamon, allspice, and salt; bring to boil. Reduce heat and simmer, stirring occasionally, about 10 minutes.

3 Whisk together milk, flour, egg, and nutmeg in small saucepan until smooth. Cook over medium heat, whisking constantly, until mixture boils and thickens, about 5 minutes. Remove from heat; stir in cheese.

4 Spray 9 x 13-inch baking dish with nonstick spray. Place 6 eggplant rounds in single layer in prepared dish; top with TVP mixture and spread evenly. Place remaining eggplant rounds evenly over TVP mixture. Top with milk mixture and spread evenly.

5 Bake, uncovered, until center is hot and edges are bubbly, about 30 minutes. Let stand 15 minutes before serving.

Per serving (⅙ of moussaka): 352 Cal, 5 g Total Fat, 2 g Sat Fat, 0 g Trans Fat, 42 mg Chol, 510 mg Sod, 37 g Carb, 17 g Sugar, 15 g Fib, 37 g Prot, 406 mg Calc.

STORE AND SERVE LATER

Prepare moussaka through step 4, but do not bake. Cover and refrigerate up to 4 days or freeze up to 3 months. If frozen, thaw the moussaka in the refrigerator overnight. To reheat, preheat the oven to 375°F. Unwrap the moussaka and bake, uncovered, until heated through, about 30 minutes. Let stand 15 minutes before serving.

Turkey-Succotash Potpie with Crispy Phyllo Crust

Turkey-Succotash Potpie with Crispy Phyllo Crust

Serves 6

- ▲ 1½ cups reduced-sodium chicken broth
- ▲ ½ cup fat-free milk
- 2 tablespoons all-purpose flour
- 2 teaspoons canola oil
- ▲ 1 onion, chopped
- 2 garlic cloves, minced
- ▲ 1 (10-ounce) package thawed frozen whole kernel corn
- ▲ 1 (10-ounce) package thawed frozen lima beans
- ▲ 2 cups cooked chopped skinless turkey breast
- ½ teaspoon salt
- 2 tablespoons chopped fresh parsley
- 6 (13 x 18-inch) sheets frozen phyllo dough, thawed

1 Preheat oven to 375°F. Spray 1½-quart baking dish with nonstick spray.

2 Whisk broth, milk, and flour in medium bowl until blended.

3 Heat oil in large nonstick skillet over medium heat. Add onion and garlic; cook, stirring occasionally, until softened, about 6 minutes. Stir in corn, lima beans, turkey and salt; cook, stirring occasionally, until heated through, about 5 minutes. Stir in broth mixture and cook, stirring constantly, until mixture boils and thickens slightly, 2–3 minutes. Stir in parsley. Pour into prepared baking dish.

4 Lightly spray 1 sheet of phyllo with nonstick spray; crumple loosely and place on top of filling. Repeat with remaining 5 sheets of phyllo. Lightly spray potpie with nonstick spray. Bake until filling is heated through and phyllo is browned, about 30 minutes. Let stand 10 minutes before serving.

Per serving (1¼ cups): 327 Cal, 5 g Total Fat, 1 g Sat Fat, 0 g Trans Fat, 63 mg Chol, 490 mg Sod, 39 g Carb, 3 g Sugar, 4 g Fib, 31 g Prot, 73 mg Calc.

STORE AND SERVE LATER
Omit step 1. Prepare the potpie through steps 2 and 3. Cover and refrigerate up to 4 days or freeze up to 4 months. If frozen, thaw the potpie in the refrigerator overnight. To reheat, preheat the oven to 375°F and proceed with step 4.

Finish With: Microwave Baked Apples, page 130

Roasted Ratatouille and White Bean Gratin Serves 4

▲ 1 (1-pound) eggplant, cut into 1-inch pieces

▲ 2 bell peppers, cut into 1-inch pieces

▲ 2 plum tomatoes, quartered

▲ 1 zucchini, cut into 1-inch pieces

▲ 1 onion, cut into 8 wedges

▲ 1 (15 ½-ounce) can cannellini beans, rinsed and drained

1/3 cup whole wheat bread crumbs

2 tablespoons grated Parmesan cheese

2 teaspoons olive oil

2 teaspoons grated lemon zest

1 teaspoon chopped fresh rosemary

1 garlic clove, minced

1 Preheat oven to 425°F. Spray large rimmed baking sheet with nonstick spray.

2 Place eggplant, bell peppers, tomatoes, zucchini, and onion on baking sheet. Lightly spray with nonstick spray and toss to coat. Spread in single layer and roast, stirring occasionally, until vegetables are browned and tender, about 30 minutes.

3 Spray 1½-quart baking dish with nonstick spray. Transfer roasted vegetables to prepared baking dish. Stir in beans.

4 Stir together bread crumbs, cheese, oil, lemon zest, rosemary, and garlic in small bowl. Sprinkle over vegetables. Bake, uncovered, until topping is browned, about 20 minutes.

Per serving (1¼ cups): 231 Cal, 4 g Total Fat, 1 g Sat Fat, 0 g Trans Fat, 2 mg Chol, 454 mg Sod, 39 g Carb, 11 g Sugar, 12 g Fib, 12 g Prot, 145 mg Calc.

5 PointsPlus® value.

STORE AND SERVE LATER

Prepare vegetable mixture through step 3. Let cool. Cover and refrigerate up to 4 days or freeze up to 3 months. If frozen, thaw overnight in refrigerator. To reheat, preheat oven to 425°F. Uncover baking dish. Prepare crumb mixture as directed in step 4. Sprinkle over vegetable mixture and bake as directed.

Pairs Well With: Kale and Apple Salad, page 87

Red Lentil and
Carrot Soup Serves 4

2	teaspoons olive oil
1	teaspoon cumin seeds
¼	teaspoon red pepper flakes
▲ 1	(32-ounce) carton reduced-sodium vegetable broth
▲ 3	carrots, thinly sliced
▲ ¾	cup red lentils
¼	teaspoon salt
1	tablespoon chopped fresh cilantro
2	teaspoons lemon juice

1 Heat oil in large saucepan over medium-high heat. Add cumin seeds and red pepper flakes; cook, stirring constantly, until fragrant, about 30 seconds. Add broth, carrots, lentils, and salt; bring to boil. Reduce heat and simmer, partially covered, until carrots and lentils are very tender, about 20 minutes.

2 Remove saucepan from heat and let soup cool 5 minutes. Puree soup in blender in batches.

3 Return soup to saucepan. Cook over medium heat, stirring occasionally, until heated through, about 2 minutes. Remove from heat and stir in cilantro and lemon juice.

Per serving (1 cup): 184 Cal, 3 g Total Fat, 0 g Sat Fat, 0 g Trans Fat, 0 mg Chol, 318 mg Sod, 29 g Carb, 5 g Sugar, 8 g Fib, 10 g Prot, 53 mg Calc.

4 PointsPlus® value

STORE AND SERVE LATER
Prepare soup through step 2. Transfer to an airtight container and let cool. Cover and refrigerate up to 4 days or freeze up to 3 months. To reheat, if frozen, thaw the soup in the refrigerator overnight. Transfer to a medium saucepan. Cover and cook over medium heat, stirring occasionally, until heated through, 8–10 minutes. Stir in 1 tablespoon chopped fresh cilantro and 2 teaspoons lemon juice.

Three Cheese Zucchini and Spinach Lasagna Serves 8

2 teaspoons olive oil

▲ 1 onion, chopped

▲ 1 zucchini, diced

▲ 1 (5-ounce) container baby spinach

▲ 1 (15-ounce) container fat-free ricotta cheese

1/2 cup shredded reduced-fat Swiss cheese

3 tablespoons grated Parmesan cheese

3/4 teaspoon salt

▲ 3 cups fat-free milk

3 tablespoons all-purpose flour

9 no-boil lasagna noodles

1 Preheat oven to 375°F. Spray 9 x 13-inch baking dish with nonstick spray.

2 Heat oil in large nonstick skillet over medium-high heat. Add onion and zucchini; cook, stirring occasionally, until lightly browned, about 8 minutes. Stir in spinach; cook, stirring constantly, until wilted, about 3 minutes. Remove from heat; let cool 5 minutes. Stir in ricotta, Swiss cheese, Parmesan cheese, and 1/2 teaspoon salt until well mixed.

3 To make sauce, whisk together milk, flour, and remaining 1/4 teaspoon salt in medium saucepan until smooth. Cook over medium heat, whisking constantly, until sauce comes to a boil and thickens, about 8 minutes.

4 Spread 1/2 cup sauce into prepared baking dish. Cover with 3 noodles, overlapping slightly as needed. Cover with half of vegetable mixture and one-third of remaining sauce. Repeat layering once with noodles, vegetable mixture, and sauce. Top with remaining noodles and remaining sauce.

5 Cover lasagna loosely with foil. Bake 45 minutes. Remove foil and bake until hot and bubbly, about 10 minutes. Let stand 10 minutes before serving.

Per serving (1/8 of lasagna): 206 Cal, 3 g Total Fat, 1 g Sat Fat, 0 g Trans Fat, 10 mg Chol, 408 mg Sod, 30 g Carb, 9 g Sugar, 2 g Fib, 16 g Prot, 388 mg Calc.

STORE AND SERVE LATER

Omit step 1. Prepare lasagna through step 4 and let cool. Cover and refrigerateup to 4 days or freeze up to 3 months. If frozen, thaw the lasagna in the refrigerator overnight. To reheat, preheat the oven to 375°F. Cover the lasagna with foil and bake 45 minutes. Remove the foil and bake until heated through, 10 minutes. Let stand 10 minutes before serving.

Polenta and Mushroom Bolognese Casserole Serves 4

1 **cup boiling water**

▲ ½ **ounce dried porcini mushrooms**

2 **teaspoons olive oil**

▲ 2 **portobello mushrooms, stems discarded, caps finely chopped**

▲ 1 **onion, chopped**

▲ 1 **carrot, chopped**

▲ 1 **celery stalk, chopped**

2 **garlic cloves, minced**

▲ 1 **cup no-salt-added canned diced tomatoes**

½ **teaspoon chopped fresh rosemary**

▲ 2 **(16-ounce) tubes fat-free polenta, cut into 24 (½-inch) slices**

¾ **cup shredded part-skim mozzarella cheese**

1 Combine boiling water and porcini mushrooms in small bowl. Let stand until mushrooms are softened, about 15 minutes. Remove mushrooms with slotted spoon to sieve; rinse mushrooms under cold running water, then coarsely chop. Reserve ½ cup mushroom soaking liquid.

2 Heat oil in large nonstick skillet over medium-high heat. Add portobello mushrooms, onion, carrot, celery, garlic, and porcini mushrooms; cook, stirring occasionally, until vegetables are very tender, about 10 minutes. Add tomatoes, rosemary, and reserved mushroom soaking liquid; bring to boil. Reduce heat, cover and simmer, stirring occasionally, until sauce thickens slightly, about 10 minutes.

3 Preheat oven to 350°F. Spray 9 x 13-inch baking dish with nonstick spray.

4 Spoon about ½ cup sauce into prepared baking dish. Place 12 polenta slices over sauce, overlapping as needed. Top with ½ cup sauce and sprinkle with half of the mozzarella. Top with remaining polenta slices. Spoon remaining sauce evenly over polenta; sprinkle with remaining mozzarella.

5 Cover with foil and bake until casserole is hot and cheese is melted, about 20 minutes. Let stand 5 minutes before serving.

Per serving (¼ of casserole): 317 Cal, 8 g Total Fat, 3 g Sat Fat, 0 g Trans Fat, 13 mg Chol, 896 mg Sod, 47 g Carb, 5 g Sugar, 5 g Fib, 14 g Prot, 214 mg Calc.

8 PointsPlus® value

STORE AND SERVE LATER
Prepare the casserole through step 4, omitting step 3 (do not bake). Let cool. Cover and refrigerate overnight or freeze up to 3 months. If frozen, thaw the casserole in the refrigerator overnight. To reheat, preheat the oven to 375°F. Unwrap casserole. Cover with foil and bake until hot and cheese is melted, 20 minutes. Let stand 5 minutes before serving.

Creamy Butternut and Penne Casserole with Ricotta Serves 6

▲ 1 **(20-ounce) package peeled cut-up butternut squash (about 4 cups)**

2 **teaspoons chopped fresh sage**

2 **teaspoons olive oil**

³/₄ **teaspoon salt**

▲ 6 **ounces whole wheat penne**

▲ 1 **(15-ounce) container fat-free ricotta cheese**

▲ ³/₄ **cup fat-free half-and-half**

¹/₈ **teaspoon ground nutmeg**

3 **tablespoons grated Parmesan cheese**

1 Preheat oven to 400°F. Spray 2-quart baking dish with nonstick spray.

2 Combine squash, sage, oil, and ¹/₄ teaspoon salt on baking sheet; toss to coat well. Spread squash mixture in single layer and roast, stirring occasionally, until squash is tender and lightly browned, about 20 minutes.

3 Reduce oven temperature to 375°F.

4 Meanwhile, bring large pot of water to boil. Add pasta and cook until just al dente, about 7 minutes. Drain pasta and return to pot. Add 1 cup ricotta, half-and-half, nutmeg, and remaining ¹/₂ teaspoon salt; stir until pasta is evenly coated. Gently stir in squash. Transfer pasta mixture to baking dish.

5 Spoon dollops of remaining ricotta over top. Sprinkle with Parmesan. Bake, uncovered, until heated through and topping is lightly browned, about 20 minutes.

Per serving (generous 1 cup): 233 Cal, 3 g Total Fat, 1 g Sat Fat, 0 g Trans Fat, 8 mg Chol, 451 mg Sod, 36 g Carb, 7 g Sugar, 5 g Fib, 15 g Prot, 334 mg Calc.

STORE AND SERVE LATER

Prepare the casserole through step 4, omitting step 3 (do not bake). Let cool. Cover and refrigerate up to 4 days. To reheat, preheat the oven to 375°F. Unwrap casserole. Spoon the remaining ricotta over top of casserole; sprinkle with 3 tablespoons grated Parmesan. Bake, uncovered, until heated through and topping is lightly browned, about 20 minutes.

Finish With: Honeyed Fruits with Toasted Almonds, page 130

**Creamy Butternut and
Penne Casserole with Ricotta**

Roasted Eggplant, Fennel, and Tomato Soup Serves 4

▲ 1 **(1-pound) eggplant, peeled and cut into 1-inch pieces**

▲ 1 **fennel bulb, thickly sliced**

▲ 1 **onion, cut into 6 wedges**

▲ 3 **plum tomatoes, each cut into 4 wedges**

4 **whole garlic cloves, peeled**

2 **teaspoons olive oil**

▲ 5 **cups reduced-sodium chicken broth**

1 **teaspoon chili powder**

¼ **teaspoon ground cinnamon**

¼ **teaspoon salt**

¼ **cup reduced-fat half-and-half**

1 Preheat oven to 450°F. Combine eggplant, fennel, onion, tomatoes, garlic, and oil in large shallow roasting pan; toss to coat. Roast, stirring occasionally, until vegetables are tender and lightly browned, about 25 minutes.

2 Transfer vegetables to large saucepan. Add broth, chili powder, cinnamon, and salt; bring to boil. Remove saucepan from heat and let soup cool 5 minutes. Puree soup in blender in batches.

3 Return soup to saucepan. Stir in half-and-half and cook over medium heat, stirring often, until heated through, about 2 minutes.

Per serving (1½ cups): 150 Cal, 5 g Total Fat, 1 g Sat Fat, 0 g Trans Fat, 0 mg Chol, 296 mg Sod, 22 g Carb, 8 g Sugar, 3 g Fib, 9 g Prot, 94 mg Calc.

STORE AND SERVE LATER

Prepare the soup through step 2. Transfer to an airtight container and let cool. Cover and refrigerate up to 4 days or freeze up to 3 months. If frozen, thaw the soup in the refrigerator overnight. Transfer to a medium saucepan. Cover and cook over medium heat, stirring occasionally, until heated through, 8–10 minutes. Stir in ¼ cup reduced-fat half-and-half and cook until heated through, about 1 minute longer.

Pairs Well With: Green Bean and Roasted Pepper Salad, page 86

Curried Vegetable Stew with Rice Serves 4

2 teaspoons canola oil

▲ 1 onion, chopped

▲ 1 red bell pepper, chopped

▲ 2 carrots, chopped

▲ 2 plum tomatoes, chopped

3 garlic cloves, minced

2 teaspoons grated peeled fresh ginger

2 teaspoons curry powder

1 teaspoon harissa

1/2 teaspoon salt

▲ 1 1/2 cups reduced-sodium chicken broth

▲ 1 large baking potato, scrubbed and cubed

▲ 1 cup thawed frozen green peas

▲ 2 cups hot cooked brown rice

1 Heat oil in large nonstick skillet over medium-high heat. Add onion, bell pepper, and carrots; cook, stirring occasionally, until vegetables are softened, about 6 minutes. Add tomatoes, and cook, stirring occasionally, until softened, about 5 minutes. Add garlic, ginger, curry powder, harissa, and salt and cook, stirring constantly, until fragrant, 30 seconds.

2 Add broth and potato and bring to boil. Reduce heat and simmer, partially covered, until potato is tender, about 12 minutes.

3 Stir in peas; simmer until heated through, about 2 minutes. Divide rice evenly among 4 bowls; ladle stew evenly over rice.

Per serving (1 cup stew with 1/2 cup rice): 286 Cal, 4 g Total Fat, 1 g Sat Fat, 0 g Trans Fat, 0 mg Chol, 388 mg Sod, 55 g Carb, 9 g Sugar, 9 g Fib, 9 g Prot, 66 mg Calc.

STORE AND SERVE LATER

Prepare the soup through step 2. Transfer to an airtight container and let cool. Cover and refrigerate up to 4 days or freeze up to 3 months. If frozen, thaw the soup in the refrigerator overnight. Transfer to a medium saucepan. Cover and cook over medium heat, stirring occasionally, until heated through, 8–10 minutes. Stir in the peas and cook until heated through, about 2 minutes longer. Serve stew over rice.

Mediterranean Fish Stew
with Fennel and Orange

Mediterranean Fish Stew with Fennel and Orange Serves 4

2 teaspoons olive oil

▲ 1 fennel bulb, halved lengthwise and thinly sliced

▲ 2 celery stalks, thinly sliced

2 shallots, sliced

2 garlic cloves, minced

▲ 2 plum tomatoes, chopped

▲ 1 (32-ounce) carton reduced-sodium chicken broth

1/2 cup dry white wine

4 3-inch strips orange zest

▲ 1 pound cod fillets, cut into 1-inch pieces

2 tablespoons anise-flavored liqueur

2 tablespoons chopped fresh flat-leaf parsley

1 Heat oil in Dutch oven over medium-high heat. Add fennel, celery, shallots, and garlic; cook, stirring occasionally, until softened, about 5 minutes. Add tomatoes and cook, stirring often, until softened, about 5 minutes. Add broth, wine, and orange zest; bring to boil. Reduce heat and simmer until slightly thickened, about 10 minutes.

2 Add cod and liqueur to Dutch oven and bring to gentle simmer over medium heat. Cook, stirring occasionally, until cod is just opaque in center, about 5 minutes. Stir in parsley just before serving.

Per serving (2 cups): 229 Cal, 5 g Total Fat, 1 g Sat Fat, 0 g Trans Fat, 43 mg Chol, 192 mg Sod, 16 g Carb, 5 g Sugar, 3 g Fib, 24 g Prot, 70 mg Calc.

STORE AND SERVE LATER

Transfer the stew to an airtight container and let cool. Cover and refrigerate up to 4 days or freeze up to 3 months. If frozen, thaw the stew in the refrigerator overnight. To reheat, transfer to a medium saucepan. Cover and cook over medium heat, stirring occasionally, until heated through, 8–10 minutes.

Finish With: Molasses-Spice Roasted Pears, page 131

Two-Dinner
Slow
Cooker
Meals

Take a few minutes to do some prep in the morning and you'll be rewarded with a delectable slow-simmered dinner to come home to—with a bonus. Each recipe makes 8 servings, so you'll have enough for two meals. Follow the instructions with each recipe for storing, reheating, and serving half of the dish and you'll have another almost effortless dinner for a different day.

Maple-Mustard Glazed Pot Roast with Winter Vegetables Serves 4 plus leftovers

5   tablespoons Dijon mustard

3   tablespoons maple syrup

1   teaspoon canola oil

1   teaspoon salt

▲ 1   (2-pound) boneless lean beef bottom round roast, trimmed

½   cup water

▲ 4   carrots, cut into 1-inch chunks

▲ 2   golden beets, peeled and cut into thin wedges

▲ 2   turnips, peeled and chopped

▲ 1½   pounds fingerling potatoes, scrubbed and left whole

Chopped fresh flat-leaf parsley, for garnish

1 Stir together mustard, maple syrup, oil, and salt in small bowl; brush beef lightly with 2 tablespoons of mustard mixture. Set aside remaining mustard mixture.

2 Spray large heavy skillet with nonstick spray and set over medium-high heat. Add roast and cook, turning occasionally, until browned, 6 minutes. Transfer beef to 6-quart slow cooker.

3 Add water to skillet; bring to boil, scraping browned bits at bottom of pan. Pour water mixture over roast. Add carrots, beets, turnips, and potatoes to slow cooker. Drizzle beef and vegetables with reserved mustard mixture. Cover and cook until beef is fork-tender, 4–5 hours on high or 8–10 hours on low.

4 Transfer beef to cutting board and cut crosswise into 2 pieces. Reserve half of beef in airtight container. Top with half of vegetables (about 3 cups) and half of cooking liquid (about 1 cup) and let cool. Cover and refrigerate up to 4 days.

5 Cut remaining piece of beef across grain into 12 slices. Serve with remaining 3 cups vegetables and remaining cooking liquid. Sprinkle with parsley.

Per serving (3 slices beef with ¾ cup vegetables and ¼ cup cooking liquid): 306 Cal, 7 g Total Fat, 2 g Sat Fat, 0 g Trans Fat, 88 mg Chol, 617 mg Sod, 27 g Carb, 9 g Sugar, 3 g Fib, 31 g Prot, 43 mg Calc.

SECOND TIME AROUND
Transfer the reserved beef and vegetables to a large skillet. Cover and cook over medium heat, stirring occasionally, until heated through, 8–10 minutes. Cut the beef across the grain into 12 slices. Serve with the vegetables and cooking liquid. Sprinkle with parsley.

Herbed Pot Roast with Leeks and Potatoes Serves 4 plus leftovers

▲ 1   **(2-pound) boneless lean beef bottom round roast, trimmed**

1   **teaspoon dried thyme**

1   **teaspoon dried rosemary**

1   **teaspoon dried marjoram**

½   **teaspoon salt**

1   **teaspoon olive oil**

▲ 6   **leeks, cleaned and sliced, white and light green parts only**

▲ 1   **pound small red potatoes, scrubbed and left whole**

6   **cloves garlic, sliced**

1 Sprinkle roast with thyme, rosemary, marjoram, and salt. Heat oil in large heavy skillet over medium-high heat. Add roast to skillet and cook, turning occasionally, until browned, 6 minutes. Transfer beef to 4-quart slow cooker.

2 Add leeks, potatoes, and garlic to slow cooker. Cover and cook until roast is fork-tender, 4–5 hours on high or 8–10 hours on low.

3 Transfer beef to cutting board and cut crosswise into 2 pieces. Reserve half of beef in airtight container; top with half of vegetables (about 3 cups) and let cool. Cover and refrigerate up to 4 days.

4 Cut remaining piece of beef across grain into 12 slices. Serve with remaining 3 cups vegetables.

Per serving (3 slices beef, ¾ cup vegetables, and 2 tablespoons cooking liquid): 283 Cal, 7 g Total Fat, 2 g Sat Fat, 0 g Trans Fat, 88 mg Chol, 204 mg Sod, 22 g Carb, 3 g Sugar, 2 g Fib, 31 g Prot, 60 mg Calc.

SECOND TIME AROUND
Transfer the reserved beef and vegetables to a large skillet. Cover and cook over medium heat, stirring occasionally, until heated through, 8–10 minutes. Add a few tablespoons of water, if needed. Cut the beef across the grain into 12 slices. Serve with the vegetables.

Pairs Well With: Roasted Brussels Sprouts with Walnuts and Lemon, page 37

Barbecue Brisket with Caramelized Onion Jam Serves 4 plus leftovers

▲ 6 **sweet onions, diced**

2 **garlic cloves, minced**

2 **tablespoons sugar**

4 **tablespoons red-wine vinegar**

1 **teaspoon salt**

1 **teaspoon canola oil**

1 **(2-pound) lean beef brisket, trimmed**

¹/₂ **cup barbecue sauce**

1 Place onions, garlic, sugar, vinegar, and salt in 4-quart oval slow cooker; stir to combine.

2 Heat oil in large heavy skillet over medium-high heat. Add beef and cook, until browned, 3–4 minutes on each side. Place beef on top of onion mixture; drizzle with barbecue sauce. Cover and cook until beef is fork-tender, 4–5 hours on high or 8–10 hours on low.

3 Transfer beef to cutting board and cut crosswise into 2 pieces. Reserve half of beef in airtight container. Top with half of onion mixture (about 2 cups) and let cool. Cover and refrigerate up to 4 days or freeze up to 3 months.

4 Cut remaining piece of beef across grain into 12 slices. Serve with remaining 2 cups onion mixture.

Per serving (3 slices beef with ¹/₂ cup onion mixture): 294 Cal, 7 g Total Fat, 2 g Sat Fat, 0 g Trans Fat, 59 mg Chol, 507 mg Sod, 27 g Carb, 19 g Sugar, 2 g Fib, 31 g Prot, 65 mg Calc.

SECOND TIME AROUND

If frozen, thaw the brisket and onion mixture in the refrigerator overnight. Transfer to a large skillet. Cover and cook over medium heat, stirring occasionally, until heated through, 8–10 minutes. Add a few tablespoons of water, if needed. Cut the beef across the grain into 12 slices. Serve the beef with the onion mixture.

Barbecue Brisket with Caramelized Onion Jam and Asparagus with Roasted Red Peppers and Capers, 36

Balsamic-Braised Brisket with Dried Apricots
Serves 4 plus leftovers

1	**(2-pound) lean beef brisket, trimmed**
3	**teaspoons coriander seeds, crushed**
2	**teaspoons pepper**
1	**teaspoon salt**
1	**teaspoon olive oil**
1/3	**cup balsamic vinegar**
▲ 2	**cups reduced-sodium beef broth**
8	**cloves garlic, sliced**
4	**bay leaves**
2	**tablespoons minced fresh thyme**
1	**cup dried apricot halves (6 ounces)**

1 Sprinkle beef with coriander seeds, pepper, and salt. Heat oil in large heavy skillet over medium-high heat. Add beef and cook until browned, 3–4 minutes on each side. Transfer beef to 4-quart oval slow cooker.

2 Add vinegar to skillet and cook, scraping browned bits at bottom of pan, until vinegar comes to boil. Add vinegar to slow cooker. Add broth, garlic, bay leaves, and thyme. Cover and cook until beef is fork-tender, 4–5 hours on high or 8–10 hours on low.

3 Transfer beef to cutting board and cut crosswise into 2 pieces. Reserve half of beef in airtight container. Place remaining beef on serving platter and keep warm.

4 Transfer liquid from slow cooker to medium saucepan. Add apricots to saucepan and cook, uncovered, over medium-high heat until liquid is reduced by half, about 15 minutes. Add half (about 1 cup) of apricot mixture to airtight container with beef and let cool. Cover and refrigerate up to 4 days or freeze up to 3 months.

5 Cut remaining beef across the grain into 8 slices. Serve with remaining 1 cup apricot mixture.

Per serving (2 slices brisket and about 1/4 cup apricots):
246 Cal, 7 g Total Fat, 2 g Sat Fat, 0 g Trans Fat, 59 mg Chol, 360 mg Sod, 14 g Carb, 11 g Sugar, 2 g Fib, 30 g Prot, 43 mg Calc.

6 PointsPlus® value

SECOND TIME AROUND
If frozen, thaw the reserved brisket and apricots in the refrigerator overnight. Transfer to a large skillet. Cover and cook over medium heat, stirring occasionally, until heated through, 8–10 minutes. Add a few tablespoons of water, if needed. Cut the beef across the grain into 8 slices. Serve the beef with the apricot mixture.

Ethiopian Spiced Flank Steak with "Roasted" Cauliflower Serves 4 plus leftovers

▲ 1 **(2-pound) lean flank steak, trimmed**

2 **tablespoons Ethiopian Berbere spice blend**

2 **teaspoons olive oil**

▲ 1 **large head cauliflower (about 2 pounds), cut into florets**

6 **cloves garlic, minced**

1 **teaspoon salt**

2 **teaspoons grated lemon zest**

1 Sprinkle steak with spice blend. (If Berbere spice blend is unavailable, substitute this combination of spices: 1 tablespoon chili powder, 2 teaspoons ground cumin, 1 teaspoon ground coriander, $1/2$ teaspoon ground ginger, and $1/2$ teaspoon black pepper). Heat 1 teaspoon oil in large heavy skillet over medium-high heat. Add steak and cook until browned, 3–4 minutes on each side. Transfer to 4-quart oval slow cooker.

2 Toss together cauliflower, garlic, salt, and remaining 1 teaspoon oil in large bowl. Add cauliflower to slow cooker. Cover and cook until steak is fork-tender, 4–5 hours on high or 8–10 hours on low.

3 Transfer steak to cutting board and cut crosswise into 2 pieces. Reserve half of steak in airtight container. Stir lemon zest into cauliflower mixture. Top steak in container with half of cauliflower mixture (about $2^2/3$ cups) and let cool. Cover and refrigerate up to 4 days.

4 Cut remaining piece of steak across grain into 12 slices, Serve with remaining $2^2/3$ cups cauliflower mixture.

Per serving (3 slices steak and $^2/3$ cup cauliflower): 206 Cal, 8 g Total Fat, 3 g Sat Fat, 0 g Trans Fat, 42 mg Chol, 371 mg Sod, 8 g Carb, 3 g Sugar, 3 g Fib, 26 g Prot, 43 mg Calc.

SECOND TIME AROUND

Transfer the reserved steak and cauliflower to a large skillet. Cover and cook over medium heat, stirring occasionally, until heated through, 8–10 minutes. Add a few tablespoons of water, if needed. Cut the steak across the grain into 12 slices. Serve the steak with the cauliflower.

Pairs Well With: Polenta with Goat Cheese and Chives, page 181

Argentine-Style Flank Steak Stuffed with Spinach

Argentine-Style Flank Steak Stuffed with Spinach Serves 4 plus leftovers

▲ 1 **(5-ounce) package baby spinach**

▲ 1 **large onion, quartered**

1/2 **cup fresh flat-leaf parsley leaves**

1/2 **cup fresh cilantro leaves**

2 **tablespoons red-wine vinegar**

4 **cloves garlic**

1 1/4 **teaspoons salt**

1 **tablespoon ground cumin**

1 **tablespoon ground coriander**

1/2 **teaspoon cayenne**

▲ 2 **carrots, cut into matchstick-thin strips**

▲ 2 **(1-pound) lean flank steaks, trimmed**

▲ 2 **tomatoes, diced**

1 Pulse spinach, onion, 1/4 cup parsley, 1/4 cup cilantro, vinegar, garlic, 1 teaspoon salt, cumin, coriander, and cayenne in food processor until mixture is finely chopped.

2 Arrange carrots evenly on steaks, leaving 1/2-inch border. Spoon spinach mixture evenly on top of carrots. Starting at one narrow end, roll up jelly-roll fashion. Tie with kitchen string at 1-inch intervals.

3 Place steak rolls in 4-quart slow cooker. Cover and cook until steak is fork-tender, 4–5 hours on high or 8–10 hours on low.

4 Just before serving, stir together tomatoes, remaining 1/4 cup parsley, remaining 1/4 cup cilantro, and remaining 1/4 teaspoon salt in medium bowl.

5 Reserve 1 steak roll and any cooking juices in airtight container and let cool. Cover and refrigerate up to 4 days or freeze up to 3 months.

6 Cut remaining steak roll into 12 slices and serve with tomato mixture.

Per serving (3 slices steak and 1/2 cup tomato mixture):
193 Cal, 7 g Total Fat, 3 g Sat Fat, 0 g Trans Fat, 42 mg Chol, 457 mg Sod, 7 g Carb, 2 g Sugar, 2 g Fib, 25 g Prot, 55 mg Calc.

5 PointsPlus© value

SECOND TIME AROUND

If frozen, thaw the reserved steak roll in the refrigerator overnight. Transfer steak roll and cooking juices to a medium skillet. Cover and cook over medium heat, turning occasionally, until heated through, 8–10 minutes. Prepare the tomato mixture as in step 4. Cut steak roll into 12 slices and serve with tomato mixture.

Pairs Well With: **Herbed Parmesan-Garlic Pasta, page 181**

Spicy Jerk Beef Stew with Plantains

Serves 4 plus leftovers

▲ 4   **cups reduced-sodium vegetable broth**

▲ 2   **pounds lean top round steak, trimmed and cut into 1-inch cubes**

   2   **tablespoons jerk seasoning**

▲ 4   **large red onions, cut into ½-inch slices**

   4   **plantains, peeled and cut into ½-inch slices**

▲ 2   **scallions, thinly sliced**

      Grated zest and juice of 1 lime

1 Bring broth to boil in medium saucepan.

2 Sprinkle beef with jerk seasoning. Place beef, onions, and plantains in 6-quart slow cooker. Add hot broth to slow cooker. Cover and cook until beef is fork-tender, 4–5 hours on high or 8–10 hours on low.

3 Just before serving, stir together scallions and lime zest and juice in small bowl.

4 Reserve half of stew (about 8 cups) in airtight container and let cool. Cover and refrigerate up to 4 days or freeze up to 3 months.

5 Ladle the remaining 8 cups stew evenly among 4 bowls; sprinkle evenly with scallion mixture.

Per serving (about 2 cups): 310 Cal, 5 g Total Fat, 2 g Sat Fat, 0 g Trans Fat, 56 mg Chol, 322 mg Sod, 38 g Carb, 18 g Sugar, 4 g Fib, 29 g Prot, 41 mg Calc.

SECOND TIME AROUND

If frozen, thaw the reserved stew in the refrigerator overnight. Transfer the stew to a medium saucepan. Cover and cook over medium heat, stirring occasionally, until heated through, 8–10 minutes. Add a few tablespoons of water, if needed. Prepare the scallion mixture as directed in step 3. Divide the stew among 4 bowls and sprinkle evenly with the scallion mixture.

Malaysian Beef Stew Serves 4 plus leftovers

1	**stalk lemongrass**
8	**cloves garlic, peeled**
4	**kaffir lime leaves or 2 teaspoons grated lime zest**
2	**tablespoons peeled chopped fresh ginger**
2	**tablespoons turmeric**
1	**teaspoon salt**
3	**cups light coconut milk**
▲ 2	**pounds lean top round steak, trimmed and cut into 1-inch cubes**
▲ 1	**pound small red potatoes, scrubbed**
1	**pound shallots, peeled and left whole**

1 Cut green top and root end off lemongrass and discard. Peel away tough outer layer from stalk and discard. Thinly slice pale inner stalk and place in food processor. Add garlic, lime leaves, ginger, turmeric, and salt and pulse until thick paste forms. (Alternately, skip this step and use 2 tablespoons prepared green curry paste). Transfer to 4-quart slow cooker.

2 Add coconut milk to slow cooker and whisk until mixture is well combined. Add steak, potatoes, and shallots. Cover and cook until beef is fork-tender, 4–5 hours on high or 8–10 hours on low.

3 Reserve half of stew (about 4 cups) in airtight container and let cool. Cover and refrigerate up to 4 days.

4 Ladle the remaining 4 cups stew evenly among 4 bowls.

Per serving (about 1 cup): 321 Cal, 11 g Total Fat, 2 g Sat Fat, 0 g Trans Fat, 56 mg Chol, 341 mg Sod, 27 g Carb, 3 g Sugar, 2 g Fib, 31 g Prot, 42 mg Calc.

SECOND TIME AROUND

Transfer the reserved stew to a medium saucepan. Cover and cook over medium heat, stirring occasionally, until heated through, 8–10 minutes. Add a few tablespoons of water, if needed. Divide the stew among 4 bowls.

Finish With: **Rum and Coconut Bananas, page 131**

Cincinnati-Style Beef Chili Serves 4 plus leftovers

2 **tablespoons paprika**

2 **tablespoons cocoa powder**

2 **teaspoons chili powder**

1 **teaspoon cinnamon**

1 **teaspoon allspice**

1 **teaspoon salt**

▲ 1¼ **pounds lean (7% fat) ground beef**

▲ 1 **(15½-ounce) can diced tomatoes**

▲ 1 **onion, diced**

8 **cloves garlic, peeled and minced**

¼ **cup apple cider vinegar**

▲ 1 **(14½ ounce) can kidney beans, rinsed and drained**

▲ 8 **ounces whole wheat spaghetti**

▲ ½ **cup diced red onion**

4 **tablespoons shredded reduced-fat Cheddar cheese**

4 **tablespoons chopped fresh cilantro**

1 Stir together paprika, cocoa, chili powder, cinnamon, allspice, and salt in small dish. Place beef in medium bowl; stir in 3 tablespoons spice mixture. Set aside remaining spice mixture.

2 Place beef in medium nonstick skillet and cook over medium heat, breaking it apart with a wooden spoon, until browned, 6–8 minutes. Transfer to 4-quart slow cooker.

3 Add tomatoes, onion, garlic, and vinegar to slow cooker. Cover and cook 4–5 hours on high or 8–10 hours on low.

4 About 20 minutes before cooking time is up, add beans and remaining spice mixture to slow cooker and stir to combine. Cook pasta according to package directions, omitting salt if desired; drain and keep warm.

5 Reserve half of chili (about 5 cups) in airtight container and let cool. Cover and refrigerate up to 4 days or freeze up to 3 months.

6 Divide spaghetti among 4 bowls; top evenly with remaining 5 cups chili. Sprinkle evenly with onion, cheese, and cilantro.

Per serving (1 cup spaghetti, 1¼ cups chili, 2 tablespoons onion, 1 tablespoon cheese, and 1 tablespoon cilantro): 301 Cal, 5 g Total Fat, 2 g Sat Fat, 0 g Trans Fat, 44 mg Chol, 488 mg Sod, 42 g Carb, 5 g Sugar, 11 g Fib, 24 g Prot, 63 mg Calc.

7 PointsPlus® value

SECOND TIME AROUND

If frozen, thaw the reserved chili in the refrigerator overnight. Prepare 8 ounces whole wheat spaghetti according to package directions. Transfer the chili to a medium saucepan. Cover and cook over medium heat, stirring occasionally, until heated through, 8–10 minutes. Add a few tablespoons of water, if needed. Divide the spaghetti among 4 bowls; top evenly with the chili. Sprinkle evenly with ½ cup diced red onion, 4 tablespoons shredded reduced-fat Cheddar cheese, and 4 tablespoons chopped fresh cilantro.

Cincinnati-Style Beef Chili

Roast Pork with Tomatillo Sauce Serves 4 plus leftovers

2	tablespoons chipotle chile powder
2	tablespoons ground cumin
1	teaspoon salt
▲ 2	pounds tomatillos, papery husks removed, halved
▲ 2	large red onions, chopped
8	cloves garlic, sliced
1	tablespoon sugar
1	teaspoon canola oil
▲ 1	(2-pound) boneless lean center-cut pork loin roast, trimmed
1/2	cup chopped fresh cilantro
	Grated zest and juice of 2 limes

1 Stir together chile powder, cumin, and salt in small bowl.

2 Combine tomatillos, onions, garlic, sugar, and half of seasoning mixture in 6-quart slow cooker; stir to mix well.

3 Heat oil in large heavy skillet over medium-high heat. Sprinkle pork with remaining spice mixture. Add pork to skillet and cook, turning occasionally, until browned on all sides, 6–8 minutes. Add pork to slow cooker. Cover and cook until pork is fork-tender, 4–5 hours on high or 8–10 hours on low.

4 Transfer pork to cutting board and cut crosswise into 2 pieces. Reserve half of pork in airtight container. Place remaining pork on serving platter and keep warm.

5 Using slotted spoon, transfer tomatillos and onions to large bowl. Transfer cooking liquid remaining in slow cooker to medium saucepan. Set over medium-high heat and bring to boil. Reduce heat to medium and cook until slightly thickened, 5 minutes. Stir liquid into tomatillo mixture. Stir in cilantro and lime zest and juice. Add half of tomatillo sauce (about 1 1/2 cups) to container with pork and let cool. Cover and refrigerate up to 4 days or freeze up to 3 months.

6 Cut remaining pork into 8 slices. Serve with remaining 1 1/2 cups sauce.

Per serving (2 slices pork with generous 1/4 cup sauce):
251 Cal, 10 g Total Fat, 3 g Sat Fat, 0 g Trans Fat, 67 mg Chol, 373 mg Sod, 15 g Carb, 8 g Sugar, 4 g Fib, 26 g Prot, 67 mg Calc.

6 PointsPlus® value

SECOND TIME AROUND
If frozen, thaw the reserved pork and sauce in the refrigerator overnight. Transfer to a medium saucepan. Cover and cook over medium heat, stirring occasionally, until heated through, 8–10 minutes. Add a few tablespoons of water, if needed. Cut the pork into 8 slices and serve with the sauce.

Latin-Style Pork with Cumin, Garlic, and Oregano Serves 4 plus leftovers

1 teaspoon canola oil

▲ 1 (2-pound) boneless lean center-cut pork loin roast, trimmed

1/2 cup chopped fresh cilantro

2 tablespoons chopped fresh oregano

2 teaspoons ground cumin

2 teaspoons ground coriander

2 teaspoons garlic powder

2 teaspoons annatto powder or 1 teaspoon turmeric

2 teaspoons red-wine vinegar

1 teaspoon salt

1 Heat oil in large heavy skillet over medium-high heat. Add pork and cook, turning occasionally, until browned on all sides, 6–8 minutes. Transfer pork to 4-quart slow cooker.

2 Stir together cilantro, oregano, cumin, coriander, garlic powder, annatto powder, vinegar, and salt in small bowl. Add cilantro mixture to slow cooker and turn pork to coat.

3 Cover and cook until pork is fork-tender, 4–5 hours on high or 8–10 hours on low.

4 Transfer pork to cutting board and cut crosswise into 2 pieces. Reserve half of pork and half of accumulated cooking liquid (about 3/4 cup) in airtight container. Cover and refrigerate up to 4 days or freeze up to 3 months.

5 Cut remaining piece of pork into 8 slices; serve with remaining cooking liquid.

Per serving (2 slices pork and about 3 tablespoons cooking liquid): 182 Cal, 8 g Total Fat, 3 g Sat Fat, 0 g Trans Fat, 67 mg Chol, 349 mg Sod, 1 g Carb, 0 g Sugar, 1 g Fib, 24 g Prot, 33 mg Calc.

4 PointsPlus® value

SECOND TIME AROUND

If frozen, thaw the reserved pork and cooking liquid in the refrigerator overnight. Transfer to a medium saucepan. Cover and cook over medium heat, stirring occasionally, until heated through, 8–10 minutes. Add a few tablespoons of water, if needed. Cut the pork into 8 slices and serve with the cooking liquid.

Pairs Well With: Orzo with Corn and Bell Pepper, page 180

Pork and Squash Stew with Harissa
Serves 4 plus leftovers

- ▲ 1½ **pounds boneless lean center-cut pork loin, trimmed and cut into 1-inch cubes**
- 4 **tablespoons smoked paprika**
- 2 **teaspoons canola oil**
- ▲ 2 **large onions, chopped**
- ▲ 8 **cups reduced-sodium chicken broth**
- ▲ 4 **celery stalks, chopped**
- ▲ 1 **medium kabocha squash (about 3 pounds), seeded and cut into 1-inch cubes**
- ½ **cup harissa paste or 4 chipotle en adobo, minced**
- 1 **teaspoon salt**

1 Sprinkle pork with 2 tablespoons paprika. Heat 1 teaspoon oil in large heavy skillet over medium-high heat. Add half of pork and cook, stirring often, until well browned, 5–6 minutes. Transfer pork to 6-quart slow cooker. Repeat with remaining oil and remaining pork.

2 Add onions to skillet and cook, stirring occasionally, until softened, 6–8 minutes. Add ½ cup of broth to skillet; cook, scraping browned bits at bottom of pan, until mixture comes to boil. Pour onion mixture over pork. Add remaining broth, celery, squash, harissa, and salt and stir to combine. Cover and cook until pork is fork-tender, 4–5 hours on high or 8–10 hours on low.

3 Reserve half of stew (about 7 cups) in airtight container and let cool. Cover and refrigerate up to 4 days or freeze up to 3 months.

4 Ladle remaining 7 cups stew evenly into 4 bowls.

Per serving (about 1 ¾ cups): 251 Cal, 9 g Total Fat, 3 g Sat Fat, 0 g Trans Fat, 50 mg Chol, 448 mg Sod, 19 g Carb, 6 g Sugar, 4 g Fib, 25 g Prot, 77 mg Calc.

SECOND TIME AROUND
If frozen, thaw the reserved stew in the refrigerator overnight. Transfer to a medium saucepan. Cover and cook over medium heat, stirring occasionally, until heated through, 8–10 minutes. Divide the stew among 4 bowls.

Pairs Well With: **Roasted Zucchini with Yogurt and Mint, page 36**

Rosemary Pork and Potato Stew with Olives
Serves 4 plus leftovers

▲ 2 pounds boneless lean center-cut pork loin, trimmed and cut into 1-inch cubes

1 teaspoon salt

1/2 teaspoon pepper

3 teaspoons olive oil

▲ 1 large onion, thinly sliced

4 cloves garlic, minced

▲ 1 1/2 pounds red baby potatoes, halved

▲ 2 large carrots, thinly sliced

▲ 2 cups reduced-sodium chicken broth

2 teaspoons chopped fresh rosemary

1/3 cup brine-cured Kalamata olives, pitted and chopped

Grated zest from 1 lemon

1 Sprinkle pork with 1/2 teaspoon salt and 1/4 teaspoon pepper. Heat 1 teaspoon oil in large heavy skillet over medium-high heat. Add half of pork and cook, stirring often, until well browned, 5–6 minutes. Transfer to plate. Repeat with 1 teaspoon remaining oil and remaining pork.

2 Add remaining 1 teaspoon oil to skillet; add onion and cook, stirring often, until softened, 5 minutes. Add garlic; cook, stirring constantly, 1 minute. Transfer onion mixture to 6-quart slow cooker. Add potatoes, carrots, broth, rosemary, remaining 1/2 teaspoon salt, and remaining 1/4 teaspoon pepper; stir to combine. Add pork to slow cooker. Cover and cook until pork is fork-tender, 4–5 hours on high or 8–10 hours on low. Stir in olives and lemon zest.

3 Reserve half of stew (about 5 cups) in airtight container and let cool. Cover and refrigerate up to 4 days.

4 Ladle remaining 5 cups stew evenly into 4 bowls.

Per serving (about 1 1/4 cups): 261 Cal, 9 g Total Fat, 2 g Sat Fat, 0 g Trans Fat, 60 mg Chol, 609 mg Sod, 18 g Total Carb, 3 g Total Sugar, 2 g Fib, 25 g Prot, 65 mg Calc.

SECOND TIME AROUND
Transfer the stew to a medium saucepan. Cover and cook over medium heat, stirring occasionally, until heated through, 8–10 minutes. Divide the stew among 4 bowls.

Salad Lovers' Sides to Serve 4

Zucchini and Feta Salad with Dill

PER SERVING

Whisk together **grated zest and juice from 1 small lemon, 1 tablespoon olive oil,** **¼ teaspoon salt,** and **¼ teaspoon black pepper** in large bowl. Add **2 zucchini, very thinly sliced** and **2 tablespoons chopped fresh dill** and toss to coat. Sprinkle with **¼ cup crumbled feta cheese.**

Green Bean and Roasted Pepper Salad

PER SERVING

Cook **¾ pound trimmed green beans** in medium saucepan of boiling water until crisp-tender, 4 minutes. Drain, cool under cold running water, and pat dry with paper towels. Whisk together **1 tablespoon olive oil, 1 tablespoon red wine vinegar, ¼ teaspoon salt,** and **¼ teaspoon black pepper** in large bowl. Add beans, **½ cup sliced roasted red peppers (not oil packed),** and **2 tablespoons chopped fresh basil;** toss to coat.

Lemony Spinach and Avocado Salad

PER SERVING

Whisk together **1 teaspoon grated lemon zest, 2 tablespoons lemon juice, 1 tablespoon olive oil, ½ teaspoon Dijon mustard, ¼ teaspoon salt,** and **⅛ teaspoon black pepper** in large bowl. Add **4 cups baby spinach, ½ avocado, pitted, peeled, and chopped,** and **¼ cup thinly sliced red onion** and toss to coat.

Sweet and Sour Broccoli Salad

PER SERVING

Whisk together **2 tablespoons white-wine vinegar, 1 tablespoon olive oil, 2 teaspoons honey, ¼ teaspoon salt,** and **⅛ teaspoon black pepper** in large bowl. Add **3 cups small broccoli florets, ½ red bell pepper, sliced, ½ small red onion, sliced, 2 tablespoons golden raisins,** and **2 tablespoons slivered almonds, toasted,** and toss to coat.

Tomato–Goat Cheese Salad with Balsamic Dressing

Thickly slice **2 large yellow tomatoes** and arrange on serving platter. Cut **1 cup grape tomatoes** in half and place in small bowl; add **2 tablespoons minced fresh basil, 1 tablespoon olive oil, 1 tablespoon balsamic vinegar, 1 garlic clove, minced, ¼ teaspoon salt,** and **⅛ teaspoon black pepper** and stir to combine. Spoon the grape tomato mixture over the sliced tomatoes. Sprinkle with **¼ cup crumbled goat cheese.**

Cranberry-Carrot Slaw

Whisk together **¼ cup plain low-fat Greek yogurt, 1 tablespoon lemon juice, 1 garlic clove, minced, ½ teaspoon salt, ½ teaspoon ground cumin,** and **¼ teaspoon ground coriander** in large bowl. Stir in **1 pound shredded carrots, ¼ cup dried cranberries,** and **2 tablespoons chopped fresh cilantro.**

Arugula and Parmesan Salad

Whisk together **2 tablespoons white-wine vinegar, 1 tablespoon olive oil, ½ teaspoon Dijon mustard, ¼ teaspoon salt,** and **⅛ teaspoon black pepper** in large bowl. Add **6 cups arugula, 1 cup halved cherry tomatoes,** and **¼ cup shredded Parmesan cheese** and toss to coat.

Kale and Apple Salad

Whisk together **1 tablespoon olive oil, 1 tablespoon apple cider vinegar, 2 teaspoons honey, ¼ teaspoon salt,** and **¼ teaspoon black pepper** in large bowl. Add **½ pound kale, stems removed and leaves thinly sliced, 1 Gala apple, cored and cut into matchstick-thin strips,** and **2 tablespoons freshly grated Parmesan cheese** and toss to coat.

Orange and Fennel Salad

Whisk together **1 tablespoon olive oil, 1 tablespoon white-wine vinegar, ¼ teaspoon salt, ¼ teaspoon ground cumin,** and **⅛ teaspoon black pepper** in small bowl. Peel and thickly slice **4 large navel oranges** and arrange on serving platter. Core and thinly slice **1 fennel bulb;** arrange on top of oranges. Drizzle with dressing.

Cucumber Salad with Miso Dressing

Whisk together **2 tablespoons white miso, 1 tablespoon rice vinegar, 1 tablespoon orange juice, 2 teaspoons honey, 1 teaspoon dark (Asian) sesame oil,** and **pinch of cayenne** in large bowl. Add **1 English (seedless) cucumber, peeled and sliced, 1 red bell pepper, thinly sliced, 1 small red onion, thinly sliced,** and **¼ cup minced fresh cilantro** and toss to coat.

Pineapple Pork Ribs with Ginger Glaze Serves 4 plus leftovers

3	**pounds pork spareribs, trimmed**
3/4	**cup unsweetened pineapple juice**
3/4	**cup orange juice**
6	**cloves garlic, minced**
3	**tablespoons peeled minced fresh ginger**
1	**teaspoon salt**
▲ 1/2	**pineapple, peeled, cored, and diced**
▲ 1	**tomato, chopped**
3	**tablespoons chopped fresh mint**
2	**teaspoons apple cider vinegar**
▲ 1/4	**serrano or jalapeno pepper, minced**
1	**teaspoon olive oil**

1 Place ribs in a 6-quart oval slow cooker. Add pineapple juice, orange juice, garlic, ginger, and 1/2 teaspoon of the salt. Cover and cook until ribs are fork-tender, 4–5 hours on high or 8–10 hours on low.

2 Reserve half of ribs in airtight container. Transfer remaining ribs to platter; cover to keep warm.

3 Transfer cooking liquid to medium saucepan. Set over medium-high heat and bring to boil. Cook until liquid is reduced to thick glaze, about 10 minutes. Transfer half of glaze (about 1/2 cup) to container with ribs and let cool. Cover and refrigerate up to 4 days.

4 Meanwhile, to make salsa, combine pineapple, tomato, mint, vinegar, serrano pepper, and oil in medium bowl. Reserve half of salsa (about 1 cup) in airtight container; cover and refrigerate up to 4 days.

5 Divide ribs among 4 plates; drizzle with remaining 1/2 cup glaze and serve with remaining 1 cup salsa.

Per serving (2 ribs, 2 tablespoons glaze, and 1/4 cup salsa):
364 Cal, 25 g Total Fat, 9 g Sat Fat, 0 g Trans Fat, 96 mg Chol, 367 mg Sod, 11 g Carb, 6 g Sugar, 1 g Fib, 24 g Prot, 54 mg Calc.

SECOND TIME AROUND
Preheat the oven to 325°F. Transfer the reserved ribs and glaze to a large baking dish; cover with foil. Bake until heated through, about 35 minutes. Divide the ribs among 4 plates; drizzle with the glaze and serve with the reserved salsa.

Pineapple Pork Ribs with Ginger Glaze and Roasted Brussel Sprouts with Walnuts and Lemon, 37

Ma-Po Pork and Tofu Serves 4 plus leftovers

1	**pound ground lean pork loin**
6	**garlic cloves, minced**
2	**tablespoons black bean sauce**
1	**tablespoon peeled minced fresh ginger**
1	**tablespoon Sriracha (hot chili sauce)**
1	**teaspoon Asian (dark) sesame oil**
1	**teaspoon reduced-sodium soy sauce**
▲ 1	**pound firm tofu, cubed**
4	**tablespoons chopped fresh cilantro**
▲ 2	**scallions, thinly sliced**

1 Cook pork in large nonstick skillet over medium heat, breaking it up with wooden spoon, until browned, about 8 minutes. Transfer pork to 2-quart slow cooker. Stir in garlic, black bean sauce, ginger, Sriracha, sesame oil, and soy sauce.

2 Cover and cook until flavors are blended, 4–5 hours on high or 8–10 hours on low. Stir in tofu during last 15 minutes of cooking.

3 Reserve half of pork and tofu (about 3 cups) in airtight container and let cool. Cover and refrigerate up to 4 days or freeze up to 3 months.

4 Divide remaining pork and tofu among 4 bowls; sprinkle evenly with cilantro and scallions.

Per serving (³/₄ cup): 136 Cal, 7 g Total Fat, 1 g Sat Fat, 0 g Trans Fat, 33 mg Chol, 119 mg Sod, 3 g Carb, 0 g Sugar, 0 g Fib, 16 g Prot, 125 mg Calc.

SECOND TIME AROUND
If frozen, thaw the reserved pork and tofu in the refrigerator overnight. Transfer to a medium saucepan. Cover and cook over medium heat, stirring occasionally, until heated through, 8–10 minutes. Add a few tablespoons of water, if needed. Divide the pork and tofu among 4 serving bowls; sprinkle evenly with 4 tablespoons chopped fresh cilantro and 2 thinly sliced scallions.

Lamb Chili with Coriander

Serves 4 plus leftovers

▲ 8   **plum tomatoes**

▲ 3   **large onions, quartered**

1   **(6-ounce) can tomato paste**

6   **cloves garlic, peeled**

2   **pounds lean ground lamb**

▲ 4   **cups reduced-sodium beef broth**

2   **tablespoons Worcestershire sauce**

1   **tablespoon chili powder**

1   **tablespoon ground coriander**

▲ 1   **(10-ounce) package frozen corn kernels, thawed**

¼   **cup chopped fresh cilantro**

1   Place tomatoes, onions, tomato paste, and garlic in food processor, in batches if necessary, and process until finely chopped; transfer mixture to 4-quart slow cooker. Add lamb, broth, Worcestershire sauce, chili powder, and coriander and stir to mix well.

2   Cover and cook until chili is thickened, 4–5 hours on high or 8–10 hours on low. Stir in corn during the last 10 minutes of cooking.

3   Reserve half of chili (about 5 cups) in airtight container and let cool. Cover and refrigerate up to 4 days or freeze up to 3 months.

4   Ladle remaining 5 cups chili evenly into 4 bowls; sprinkle evenly with cilantro.

Per serving (about 1¼ cups): 260 Cal, 8 g Total Fat, 3 g Sat Fat, 0 g Trans Fat, 64 mg Chol, 312 mg Sod, 22 g Carb, 7 g Sugar, 3 g Fib, 26 g Prot, 50 mg Calc.

SECOND TIME AROUND

If frozen, thaw the reserved chili in the refrigerator overnight. Transfer to a medium saucepan. Cover and cook over medium heat, stirring occasionally, until heated through, 8–10 minutes. Add a few tablespoons of water, if needed. Divide the chili among 4 bowls; sprinkle evenly with cilantro.

Finish With: Browned Butter Pineapple Sundaes, page 131

Leg of Lamb Infused with Rosemary and Lemon and Minted Green Beans with Pine Nuts, 37

Leg of Lamb Infused with Rosemary and Lemon

Serves 4 plus leftovers

6   **cloves garlic, minced**

2   **tablespoons fresh rosemary leaves**

2   **tablespoons grated lemon zest**

1½ **tablespoons ground cumin**

1   **teaspoon salt**

▲ 1 **(3-pound) bone-in lean leg of lamb, trimmed**

¼ **cup lemon juice**

2   **teaspoons olive oil**

▲ 1 **large red onion, thinly sliced**

1 Stir together garlic, rosemary, lemon zest, cumin, and salt in small bowl. Rub all over lamb. Place lamb in large zip-close plastic bag. Add lemon juice and oil; seal bag and turn to coat. Refrigerate at least 4 hours or up to overnight.

2 Remove lamb from marinade; discard marinade. Place onion in 6-quart oval slow cooker; add lamb. Cover and cook until lamb is fork-tender, 4–5 hours on high or 8–10 hours on low.

3 Transfer lamb to cutting board; cover and let stand 10 minutes. Cut lamb into about 32 slices. Discard bone. Reserve half of lamb and half of onion mixture (about 1 cup) in airtight container and let cool. Cover and refrigerate up to 4 days or freeze up to 3 months.

4 Divide remaining lamb and remaining 1 cup onion mixture among 4 plates.

Per serving (about 4 slices lamb and about ¼ cup onion mixture): 212 Cal, 11 g Total Fat, 4 g Sat Fat, 0 g Trans Fat, 89 mg Chol, 365 mg Sod, 4 g Carb, 1 g Sugar, 1 g Fib, 24 g Prot, 33 mg Calc.

5 PointsPlus® value

SECOND TIME AROUND

If frozen, thaw the reserved lamb and onion mixture in the refrigerator overnight. Transfer to a medium skillet. Cover and cook over medium heat, stirring occasionally, until heated through, 8–10 minutes. Add a few tablespoons of water, if needed. Divide the lamb and onion mixture among 4 plates.

Lemon-Tarragon Chicken with Zucchini Salad Serves 4 plus leftovers

10	tarragon sprigs
1	lemon, sliced and seeded
6	garlic cloves, crushed
1	whole chicken (about 4 pounds), cut into 8 pieces
2	teaspoons canola oil
3/4	teaspoon salt
▲ 4	medium zucchini, cut into thin lengthwise slices with vegetable peeler
1/4	cup minced fresh flat-leaf parsley
2	tablespoons lemon juice

1 Place 5 tarragon sprigs, lemon, and garlic in 6-quart oval slow cooker. Rub chicken with oil and sprinkle with $1/2$ teaspoon salt.

2 Place chicken in slow cooker. Cover and cook until instant-read thermometer inserted into chicken registers 165°F, 3–4 hours on high or 6–8 hours on low.

3 Just before serving, chop remaining 5 sprigs tarragon; place in medium bowl. Add zucchini, parsley, lemon juice, and remaining $1/4$ teaspoon salt and toss to combine.

4 Remove chicken from slow cooker. Remove and discard tarragon sprigs, lemon slices, and garlic. Remove and discard skin and reserve half of chicken in airtight container. Let cool. Cover and refrigerate up to 4 days.

5 Divide remaining chicken evenly among 4 plates. Serve with zucchini salad.

Per serving ($1/8$ of chicken and $3/4$ cup salad): 163 Cal, 5 g Total Fat, 1 g Sat Fat, 0 g Trans Fat, 76 mg Chol, 314 mg Sod, 6 g Carb, 2 g Sugar, 2 g Fib, 25 g Prot, 44 mg Calc.

SECOND TIME AROUND
Prepare a fresh zucchini salad as directed in step 3. Transfer the reserved chicken to a medium saucepan. Add $1/4$ cup reduced-sodium chicken broth or water. Cover and cook over medium heat, turning occasionally, until heated through, 8–10 minutes. Divide the chicken among 4 plates. Serve the chicken with the zucchini salad.

Orange-Ginger Chicken and Butternut Squash Stew Serves 4 plus leftovers

2	pounds skinless, boneless chicken thighs, trimmed and cut into 2-inch pieces
2	teaspoons pepper
1	teaspoon canola oil
▲ 3	carrots, quartered lengthwise and cut into 1/2-inch pieces
▲ 3	stalks celery, cut in 1/2-inch slices
▲ 2	large onions, chopped
▲ 2	cups reduced-sodium chicken broth
3	tablespoons ground ginger
	Grated zest and juice of 2 oranges
1	teaspoon salt
▲ 1	large butternut squash (about 3½ pounds), peeled, seeded, and cut into 1-inch cubes

1 Sprinkle chicken with pepper. Heat oil in large heavy skillet over medium-high heat. Add chicken and cook, turning often, until well browned, 5–6 minutes. Transfer to 6-quart slow cooker.

2 Add carrots, celery, and onions to skillet. Cook, stirring occasionally, until softened, 6–8 minutes. Add 1/2 cup of broth to skillet; cook, scraping browned bits at bottom of pan, until mixture comes to boil. Pour vegetable mixture over chicken. Add ginger, orange zest, orange juice, and salt and stir to combine. Add squash to slow cooker. Cover and cook until chicken and vegetables are fork-tender, 3–4 hours on high or 6–8 hours on low.

3 Reserve half of stew (about 6 cups) in airtight container and let cool. Cover and refrigerate up to 4 days or freeze up to 4 months.

4 Ladle remaining 6 cups stew evenly into 4 bowls.

Per serving (1½ cups): 290 Cal, 10 g Total Fat, 3 g Sat Fat, 0 g Trans Fat, 74 mg Chol, 424 mg Sod, 29 g Carb, 8 g Sugar, 7 g Fib, 24 g Prot, 117 mg Calc.

SECOND TIME AROUND
If frozen, thaw the reserved stew in the refrigerator overnight. Transfer to a medium saucepan. Cover and cook over medium heat, stirring occasionally, until heated through, 8–10 minutes. Add a few tablespoons of water, if needed. Divide the stew among 4 bowls.

Pairs Well With: Zucchini and Feta Salad with Dill, page 86

Lemon-Caper Stuffed Chicken in Tomato-Herb Sauce Serves 4 plus leftovers

▲ 8 **tomatoes, halved horizontally**

1 **tablespoon chopped fresh oregano or 1½ teaspoons dried**

⅛ **teaspoon salt**

½ **cup minced fresh parsley**

3 **tablespoons capers, drained**

1 **tablespoon grated lemon zest**

▲ 8 **(¼-pound) skinless, boneless chicken breasts**

2 **tablespoons lemon juice**

Chopped fresh oregano

Grated lemon zest

Lemon wedges

1 Place tomatoes in 4-quart slow cooker. Sprinkle with oregano and salt. Stir together parsley, capers, and lemon zest in small bowl; set aside.

2 Place chicken between sheets of plastic wrap. Using meat mallet, pound chicken to ¼-inch thickness.

3 Spoon parsley mixture evenly on top of each piece of chicken; roll chicken up to enclose filling. Secure rolls with wooden toothpicks. Place seam side down, in slow cooker. Cover and cook until chicken is fork-tender, 3–4 hours on high or 6–8 hours on low.

4 Using slotted spoon, reserve 4 chicken breasts and 8 tomato halves in airtight container. Transfer remaining chicken and tomatoes to serving platter; cover to keep warm.

5 Transfer cooking juices in slow cooker to medium saucepan; set over medium-high heat and cook until thickened, about 5 minutes. Add half of cooking juices (about 1 cup) to airtight container and let cool. Cover and refrigerate up to 4 days.

6 Drizzle chicken and tomatoes on platter with remaining 1 cup cooking juices and lemon juice. Sprinkle with chopped fresh oregano and grated lemon zest. Serve with lemon wedges.

Per serving (1 chicken breast, 2 tomato halves and, ¼ cup sauce): 148 Cal, 3 g Total Fat, 1 g Sat Fat, 0 g Trans Fat, 63 mg Chol, 195 mg Sod, 6 g Carb, 3 g Sugar, 2 g Fib, 24 g Prot, 34 mg Calc.

SECOND TIME AROUND

Transfer the reserved chicken, tomatoes, and cooking juices to a large skillet. Cover and cook over medium heat, stirring occasionally, until heated through, 8–10 minutes. Divide chicken, tomatoes, and cooking juices among 4 plates. Drizzle evenly with 2 tablespoons lemon juice.

**Lemon-Caper Stuffed Chicken
in Tomato-Herb Sauce**

Braised Chicken with Green Lentils Serves 4 plus leftovers

▲ 3   **cups reduced-sodium chicken broth**

1   **cup dry white wine**

16   **shallots, halved lengthwise**

▲ 1   **cup French green lentils, picked over and rinsed**

4   **cloves garlic, sliced**

2   **tablespoons dried herbes de Provence**

2   **tablespoons Dijon mustard**

1   **teaspoon salt**

8   **skinless whole chicken legs, trimmed**

1 Combine broth, wine, shallots, lentils, garlic, herbes de Provence, mustard, and salt in 6-quart slow cooker; stir to mix well. Add chicken.

2 Cover and cook until chicken is fork-tender, 3–4 hours on high or 6–8 hours on low.

3 Reserve 4 chicken legs and half (about 2 cups) of lentil mixture in airtight container and let cool. Cover and refrigerate up to 4 days.

4 Divide remaining 4 chicken legs and 1 cup lentil mixture among 4 plates.

Per serving (1 chicken leg and ¹/₂ cup lentil mixture): 344 Cal, 9 g Total Fat, 2 g Sat Fat, 0 g Trans Fat, 89 mg Chol, 504 mg Sod, 27 g Carb, 3 g Sugar, 4 g Fib, 34 g Prot, 50 mg Calc.

SECOND TIME AROUND
Transfer the reserved chicken and lentils to a large skillet. Cover and cook over medium heat, stirring occasionally, until heated through, 8–10 minutes. Add a few tablespoons of water, if needed. Divide the chicken legs and lentils among 4 plates.

Pairs Well With: Buttery Crumb-Topped Cauliflower, page 37

Chicken with Lemongrass and Chiles
Serves 4 plus leftovers

1	stalk lemongrass
6	cloves garlic, crushed
4	shallots, peeled
▲ 3	Thai chiles or other small hot peppers, halved lengthwise and seeded
2	tablespoons chopped peeled fresh ginger
2	tablespoons Asian fish sauce
2	teaspoons turmeric
8	(¼-pound) skinless boneless chicken thighs, trimmed
4	tablespoons chopped fresh basil
▲ 2	scallions, thinly sliced

1 Cut green top and root end off lemongrass and discard. Peel away tough outer layer from remaining stalk and discard. Thinly slice pale inner stalk and place in food processor. Add garlic, shallots, chiles, ginger, fish sauce, and 1 teaspoon turmeric; pulse until thick paste forms.

2 Place chicken in 4-quart slow cooker; add lemongrass mixture and turn to coat. Cover and cook until chicken is fork-tender, 3–4 hours on high or 6–8 hours on low. Add remaining 1 teaspoon turmeric and stir until well combined.

3 Reserve 4 chicken thighs in airtight container and let cool. Cover and refrigerate up to 4 days or freeze up to 4 months.

4 Divide remaining 4 chicken thighs among 4 plates; sprinkle with basil and scallions.

Per serving (1 chicken thigh): 191 Cal, 9 g Total Fat, 2 g Sat Fat, 0 g Trans Fat, 74 mg Chol, 421 mg Sod, 6 g Carb, 2 g Sugar, 1 g Fib, 22 g Prot, 30 mg Calc.

SECOND TIME AROUND

If frozen, thaw the reserved chicken in the refrigerator overnight. Transfer to a medium skillet. Cover and cook over medium heat, turning occasionally, until heated through, 8–10 minutes. Add a few tablespoons of water, if needed. Divide the chicken thighs among 4 plates; sprinkle evenly with 4 tablespoons chopped fresh basil and 2 thinly sliced scallions.

Chicken Tikka Masala Serves 4 plus leftovers

8	skinless boneless chicken thighs
▲ 4	plum tomatoes
▲ 2	large onions, quartered
4	cloves garlic
2	tablespoons curry powder
1	tablespoon peeled coarsely chopped fresh ginger
¹/₂	tablespoon paprika
¹/₂	tablespoon ground cumin
1	teaspoon salt
▲ 1	cup plain fat-free yogurt
¹/₄	cup chopped fresh cilantro

1 Place chicken thighs in 4-quart slow cooker.

2 Puree tomatoes, onions, garlic, curry powder, ginger, paprika, cumin, and salt in food processor or blender, in batches if necessary. Add mixture to slow cooker. Cover and cook until chicken is fork-tender, 3–4 hours on high or 6–8 hours on low.

3 Turn off slow cooker. Stir in yogurt and cilantro. Reserve 4 chicken thighs and 2 cups of sauce in an airtight container and let cool. Cover and refrigerate up to 4 days.

4 Divide remaining 4 chicken thighs and remaining 2 cups sauce among 4 plates.

Per serving (1 chicken thigh and ¹/₂ cup sauce): 310 Cal, 12 g Total Fat, 3 g Sat Fat, 0 g Trans Fat, 100 mg Chol, 729 mg Sod, 17 g Carb, 10 g Sugar, 3 g Fib, 33 g Prot, 181 mg Calc.

SECOND TIME AROUND
Transfer the reserved chicken and sauce to a large skillet. Cover and cook over low heat, stirring occasionally, until heated through, 10–12 minutes. Add a few tablespoons of water, if needed. Divide the chicken thighs and sauce among 4 plates.

Pairs Well With: Minted Green Beans with Pine Nuts, page 37

Southwestern Chicken and Black Bean Meatloaf Serves 4 plus leftovers

▲ 1½ **pounds ground skinless chicken breast**

8 **ounces prepared cornbread, crumbled**

▲ 4 **large eggs, lightly beaten**

▲ 1 **(15 ½-ounce) can black beans, rinsed and drained**

▲ 1 **(10-ounce) bag frozen corn kernels**

▲ 1 **large onion, chopped**

▲ 2 **jalapeno peppers, seeded and minced**

8 **garlic cloves, minced**

1 **tablespoon ground cumin**

2 **teaspoons chipotle chile powder**

1 **teaspoon salt**

▲ ½ **cup fat-free salsa**

4 **tablespoons low-fat sour cream**

1 Spray 4-quart oval slow cooker with nonstick spray. Line slow cooker with foil, folding corners over to make handles for removing meatloaf. Spray foil with nonstick spray.

2 Combine chicken, cornbread, eggs, beans, corn, onion, jalapeno, garlic, cumin, chili powder, and salt in large bowl, mixing until blended. Transfer mixture to slow cooker and shape into loaf. Cover and cook until instant read thermometer inserted in center of loaf registers 165°F, 3–4 hours on high or 6–8 hours on low.

3 Using foil handles, transfer meatloaf to cutting board and let stand 5 minutes. Cut meatloaf in half. Reserve half of meat-loaf in airtight container and let cool. Cover and refrigerate up to 4 days or freeze up to 4 months.

4 Cut remaining half of meatloaf into 8 slices. Divide meatloaf evenly among 4 plates; top each serving with 2 tablespoons salsa and 1 tablespoon sour cream.

Per serving (2 slices meatloaf, 2 tablespoons salsa, and 1 tablespoon sour cream): 321 Cal, 8 g Total Fat, 2 g Sat Fat, 0 g Trans Fat, 169 mg Chol, 792 mg Sod, 33 g Carb, 2 g Sugar, 4 g Fib, 27 g Prot, 135 mg Calc.

8 PointsPlus® value

SECOND TIME AROUND

If frozen, thaw the meatloaf in the refrigerator overnight. Preheat the oven to 325°F. Transfer the meatloaf to small baking dish; cover with foil. Bake until heated through, about 35 minutes. Alternatively, transfer to a microwavable dish, cover with wax paper, and microwave on High until heated through, 5–6 minutes. Cut the meatloaf into 8 slices. Divide the meatloaf among 4 plates; top each serving with 2 tablespoons salsa and 1 tablespoon sour cream.

Chicken Pepperonata

Chicken Pepperonata Serves 4 plus leftovers

1 teaspoon canola oil

▲ 4 red or yellow bell peppers, cut into 1-inch strips

▲ 2 large onions, chopped

8 cloves garlic, minced

▲ 4 Peppadew peppers or other pickled cherry peppers, not packed in oil, halved

2 tablespoons fennel seed, crushed

1 teaspoon salt

1 teaspoon black pepper

8 (¼-pound) chicken drumsticks, skinned

▲ 1⅓ cups pearl barley

1 Heat oil in large skillet over medium-high heat. Add bell peppers, skin side down, and cook until skins are browned, 5–6 minutes. Transfer peppers to 6-quart slow cooker.

2 Add onions to same skillet and cook, stirring often, until softened and browned, 5–6 minutes. Transfer to slow cooker.

3 Add garlic, peppadew peppers, fennel seed, salt, and black pepper to slow cooker and stir to combine. Add drumsticks to slow cooker. Cover and cook until chicken is fork-tender, 3–4 hours on high or 6–8 hours on low.

4 About 40 minutes before cooking time is up, cook barley according to package directions.

5 Reserve 4 drumsticks and half of pepper mixture (about 2 cups) in airtight container and let cool. Reserve half of barley (about 2 cups) in separate airtight container and let cool. Cover and refrigerate up to 4 days.

6 Divide remaining 4 chicken drumsticks, remaining 2 cups pepper mixture, and remaining 2 cups barley among 4 plates.

Per serving (1 drumstick, ½ cup pepper mixture, and ½ cup barley): 249 Cal, 4 g Total Fat, 1 g Sat Fat, 0 g Trans Fat, 40 mg Chol, 202 mg Sod, 36 g Carb, 4 g Sugar, 8 g Fib, 17 g Prot, 52 mg Calc.

6 PointsPlus value

SECOND TIME AROUND

Transfer the reserved drumsticks and pepper mixture to a medium skillet. Cover and cook over medium heat, stirring occasionally, until heated through, 8–10 minutes. Add a few tablespoons of water, if needed. Transfer the reserved barley to a medium microwavable dish, cover with wax paper, and microwave on high until heated through, 2–3 minutes. Divide the chicken, pepper mixture, and barley among 4 plates.

Turkey and White Bean Chili

Serves 4 plus leftovers

▲ 1 **cup dried navy beans, picked over, rinsed, and drained**

▲ 1 **pound ground skinless turkey breast**

▲ 4 **cups reduced-sodium chicken broth**

▲ 1½ **cups fat-free green salsa**

4 **cloves garlic, minced**

▲ 2 **onions, coarsely chopped**

2 **tablespoons chili powder**

2 **tablespoons ground cumin**

▲ 1 **jalapeño pepper, minced**

³/₄ **teaspoon salt**

4 **tablespoons shredded reduced-fat Monterey Jack cheese**

1 Combine beans and enough water to cover by 3 inches in large bowl. Let stand overnight; drain. Combine beans and enough water to cover by 1 inch in large saucepan. Bring to boil over medium-high heat. Reduce heat and cook beans 10 minutes. Drain and place in 4-quart slow cooker.

2 Meanwhile, spray medium nonstick skillet with nonstick spray and set over medium heat. Add turkey and cook, breaking it up with wooden spoon, until browned, 5 minutes.

3 Add turkey, broth, 1 cup of salsa, garlic, onions, chili powder, cumin, jalapeño, and salt to slow cooker. Cover and cook until beans are tender, 3–4 hours on high or 6–8 hours on low. Reserve half of chili (about 6 cups) in airtight container and let cool. Cover and refrigerate up to 4 days or freeze up to 4 months.

4 Ladle remaining 6 cups chili evenly into 4 bowls; top each serving with 2 tablespoons remaining salsa and 1 tablespoon cheese.

Per serving (1 bowl): 171 Cal, 3 g Total Fat, 1 g Sat Fat, 0 g Trans Fat, 26 mg Chol, 626 mg Sod, 16 g Carb, 4 g Sugar, 4 g Fib, 21 g Prot, 150 mg Calc.

SECOND TIME AROUND

If frozen, thaw the reserved chili in the refrigerator overnight. Transfer to a medium saucepan. Cover and cook over medium heat, stirring occasionally, until heated through, 8–10 minutes. Add a few tablespoons of water, if needed. Divide the chili among 4 bowls; top each serving with 2 tablespoons fat-free green salsa and 1 tablespoon shredded reduced-fat Monterey Jack cheese.

Turkey Sausages with Cabbage and Apples
Serves 4 plus leftovers

▲ 1   large head savoy cabbage (about 3 pounds), thinly sliced

▲ 1   (32-ounce) container reduced-sodium sauerkraut, drained

▲ 4   Fuji apples, cored and cut into eighths

4   cloves garlic, crushed

▲ 2   onions, chopped

10   whole juniper berries

2   (2-inch) cinnamon sticks

8   whole cloves

20   whole black peppercorns

2   pounds reduced-fat turkey sausage links

1 Place cabbage, sauerkraut, apples, garlic, and onions in 7-quart slow cooker and stir to combine.

2 Tie juniper berries, cinnamon sticks, cloves, and peppercorns in cheesecloth bag; add to slow cooker.

3 Spray large nonstick skillet with nonstick spray and set over medium heat. Add sausages and cook, turning often, until well browned, 6–8 minutes. Add to slow cooker. Cover and cook until sausages and vegetables are tender, 3–4 hours on high or 6–8 hours on low. Remove and discard cheesecloth bag.

4 Reserve half of sausage links and half of cabbage mixture (about 5 cups) in airtight container and let cool. Cover and refrigerate up to 4 days or freeze up to 3 months.

5 Divide remaining sausage links and cabbage mixture among 4 plates.

Per serving (about 3 ounces sausage and 1¼ cups cabbage mixture): 286 Cal, 9 g Total Fat, 3 g Sat Fat, 0 g Trans Fat, 49 mg Chol, 923 mg Sod, 35 g Carb, 14 g Sugar, 10 g Fib, 19 g Prot, 129 mg Calc.

7 PointsPlus® value

SECOND TIME AROUND
If frozen, thaw the reserved sausages and cabbage mixture in the refrigerator overnight. Transfer to a medium skillet. Cover and cook over medium heat, stirring occasionally, until heated through, 8–10 minutes. Add a few tablespoons of water, if needed. Divide the sausages and cabbage mixture among 4 plates.

Finish With: **Maple-Mint Fruit Compote, page 130**

Turkey Pasta Fagioli   Serves 4 plus leftovers

▲ 1   cup dried kidney beans, picked over, rinsed, and drained

▲ 1   pound ground skinless turkey breast

10   sprigs thyme

5   sprigs rosemary

4   bay leaves

▲ 2   large onions, chopped

6   cloves garlic, minced

▲ 4   cups reduced-sodium chicken broth

▲ 1   (28-ounce) can whole Italian tomatoes, chopped

1   teaspoon salt

▲ 12   ounces whole wheat orrechiette or other small pasta

1 Combine beans and enough water to cover by 3 inches in large bowl. Let stand overnight; drain. Combine beans and enough water to cover by 1 inch in large saucepan. Bring to boil over medium-high heat. Reduce heat and cook beans 10 minutes. Drain and place in 4-quart slow cooker.

2 Meanwhile, spray medium nonstick skillet with nonstick spray and set over medium heat. Add turkey and cook, breaking it up with wooden spoon, until browned, 5 minutes. Add to slow cooker.

3 Tie thyme, rosemary, and bay leaves in cheesecloth bag; add to slow cooker. Add onions, garlic, broth, tomatoes, and salt to slow cooker. Cover and cook until beans are tender, 6–8 hours on high or 8–10 hours on low. Twenty minutes before serving, add pasta to slow cooker and cook on high until tender, about 20 minutes. Remove and discard cheesecloth bag.

4 Reserve half of soup (about 5 cups) in airtight container and let cool. Cover and refrigerate up to 4 days.

5 Ladle remaining 5 cups soup evenly into 4 bowls.

Per serving (about 1¼ cups): 347 Cal, 3 g Total Fat, 0 g Sat Fat, 0 g Trans Fat, 23 mg Chol, 581 mg Sod, 54 g Carb, 6 g Sugar, 9 g Fib, 28 g Prot, 69 mg Calc.

SECOND TIME AROUND
Transfer the reserved soup to a medium saucepan. Cover and cook over medium heat, stirring occasionally, until heated through, 8–10 minutes. Divide the soup among 4 bowls.

Pairs Well With: Sweet and Sour Broccoli Salad, page 86

Turkey Pasta Fagioli

Shrimp Gumbo Serves 4 plus leftovers

▲ **4** cups fish broth

▲ **4** stalks celery, cut into 1-inch chunks

▲ **2** tomatoes, quartered

▲ **2** (14 1/2-ounce) cans no-salt-added diced tomatoes

▲ **1** pound okra, trimmed and cut into 1/2-inch slices

▲ **1** pound green beans, trimmed and halved

4 cloves garlic, sliced

1/2 cup bottled clam juice

2 tablespoons Worcestershire sauce

2 tablespoons ground cumin

1 tablespoon minced fresh thyme

2 teaspoons minced fresh oregano

▲ **1** pound medium peeled, deveined shrimp

1/4 cup minced fresh flat-leaf parsley

1 Combine broth, celery, tomatoes, okra, beans, garlic, clam juice, Worcestershire sauce, cumin, thyme, and oregano in 4-quart slow cooker. Cover and cook until vegetables are fork-tender, 3–4 hours on high or 6–8 hours on low.

2 About 30 minutes before cooking time is up, add shrimp to slow cooker. Cover and cook on high until shrimp are just opaque in center, about 25 minutes. Stir in parsley.

3 Reserve half of gumbo (about 6½ cups) in airtight container and let cool. Cover and refrigerate up to 4 days or freeze up to 3 months.

4 Ladle remaining 6½ cups gumbo evenly into 4 bowls.

Per serving (about 1²/₃ cups): 141 Cal, 2 g Total Fat, 0 g Sat Fat, 84 g Trans Fat, 84 mg Chol, 616 mg Sod, 17 g Carb, 6 g Sugar, 6 g Fib, 15 g Prot, 172 mg Calc.

SECOND TIME AROUND

If frozen, thaw the reserved gumbo in the refrigerator overnight. Transfer to a medium saucepan. Cover and cook over medium heat, stirring occasionally, until heated through, 8–10 minutes. Divide the gumbo among 4 bowls.

Moroccan Chickpea Stew

Serves 4 plus leftovers

▲ 2 **(14-ounce) cans diced tomatoes**

▲ 2 **large onions, quartered**

8 **cloves garlic, peeled**

1 **tablespoon fresh oregano leaves or 1½ teaspoons dried**

▲ 8 **cups reduced-sodium vegetable broth**

▲ 2 **(15 ½-ounce) cans chickpeas, rinsed and drained**

2 **whole dried Ancho chiles**

2 **tablespoons ground cumin**

1 **tablespoon paprika**

1½ **teaspoons ground cinnamon**

½ **cup chopped fresh cilantro**

2 **tablespoons toasted sesame seeds**

1 Puree tomatoes, onions, garlic, and oregano in food processor or blender, in batches if necessary. Transfer to 6-quart slow cooker. Stir in broth, chickpeas, chiles, cumin, paprika, and cinnamon. Cover and cook until onions are tender, 3–4 hours on high or 6–8 hours on low.

2 Remove and discard chiles. Stir in cilantro. Reserve half of stew (about 7 cups) in airtight container and let cool. Cover and refrigerate up to 4 days or freeze up to 3 months.

3 Ladle remaining 7 cups stew evenly into 4 bowls. Sprinkle evenly with sesame seeds.

Per serving (about 1¾ cups stew and ½ tablespoon sesame seeds): 183 Cal, 3 g Total Fat, 0 g Sat Fat, 0 g Trans Fat, 0 mg Chol, 616 mg Sod, 31 g Carb, 8 g Sugar, 8 g Fib, 7 g Prot, 96 mg Calc.

4 PointsPlus® value

SECOND TIME AROUND

If frozen, thaw the reserved stew in the refrigerator overnight. Transfer to a medium saucepan. Cover and cook over medium heat, stirring occasionally, until heated through, 8–10 minutes. Add a few tablespoons of water, if needed. Divide the stew among 4 bowls; sprinkle evenly with 2 tablespoons sesame seeds.

Pairs Well With: **Orange and Fennel Salad, page 87**

**Barley Risotto with Shrimp
and Wild Mushrooms**

Barley Risotto with Shrimp and Wild Mushrooms Serves 4 plus leftovers

▲ 1 ounce dried porcini mushrooms

▲ 5 cups reduced-sodium vegetable broth

▲ 2 cups pearl barley, rinsed

▲ 3 celery stalks, chopped

▲ 2 large onions, chopped

▲ 2 carrots, cut into ½-inch slices

▲ 1 pound mixed fresh mushrooms, halved

  6 cloves garlic, minced

  2 teaspoons salt

▲ 1 pound medium peeled, deveined shrimp

  4 tablespoons shaved Parmesan cheese

1 Place dried mushrooms in food processor and pulse until coarsely ground. Transfer to 6-quart slow cooker. Add broth, barley, celery, onions, carrots, mushrooms, garlic, and salt and stir to combine. Cover and cook until barley is tender, 4–6 hours on low.

2 About 30 minutes before cooking time is up, add shrimp to slow cooker. Cover and cook on high until shrimp are just opaque in center, about 25 minutes. Stir in 2 tablespoons of the cheese. Reserve half of risotto (about 5½ cups) in airtight container and let cool. Cover and refrigerate up to 4 days.

3 Divide remaining risotto among 4 bowls; sprinkle evenly with remaining 2 tablespoons cheese.

Per serving (1⅓ cups): 294 Cal, 2 g Total Fat, 1 g Sat Fat, 0 g Trans Fat, 86 mg Chol, 847 mg Sod, 51 g Carb, 5 g Sugar, 11 g Fib, 18 g Prot, 108 mg Calc.

SECOND TIME AROUND

Transfer the reserved risotto to large microwavable dish, cover with wax paper, and microwave on High, stirring occasionally, until heated through, 6–8 minutes. Divide the risotto among 4 bowls; sprinkle evenly with 2 tablespoons shaved Parmesan.

Pairs Well With: **Asparagus with Roasted Peppers and Capers, page 36**

Indian Lentil Stew Serves 4 plus leftovers

1	tablespoon ground ginger
1	tablespoon paprika
2	teaspoons ground cumin
2	teaspoons turmeric
1	teaspoon salt
▲ 6	cups reduced-sodium vegetable broth
▲ 1½	cups split mung beans or yellow or red lentils, picked over, rinsed, and drained
▲ 2	large onions, chopped
8	cloves garlic, minced

1 Stir together ginger, paprika, cumin, turmeric, and salt in small bowl.

2 Combine broth, beans, onions, and garlic in 4-quart slow cooker; stir in 2 tablespoons of the spice mixture. Cover and cook until beans are tender, 4–5 hours on high or 8–10 hours on low. Stir in remaining spice mixture.

3 Reserve half of stew (about 4 cups) in airtight container and let cool. Cover and refrigerate up to 4 days or freeze up to 3 months.

4 Ladle remaining 4 cups stew evenly into 4 bowls.

Per serving (about 1 cup): 173 Cal, 1 g Total Fat, 0 g Sat Fat, 0 g Trans Fat, 0 mg Chol, 406 mg Sod, 32 g Carb, 6 g Sugar, 8 g Fib, 10 g Prot, 87 mg Calc.

SECOND TIME AROUND
If frozen, thaw the reserved stew in the refrigerator overnight. Transfer to a medium saucepan. Cover and cook over medium heat, stirring occasionally, until heated through, 8–10 minutes. Divide the stew among 4 bowls.

Pairs Well With: Lemony Spinach and Avocado Salad, page 86

Two-Pea Soup with Pumpernickel Croutons Serves 4 plus leftovers

▲ 2 **cups dried yellow split peas, picked over, rinsed, and drained**

▲ 3 **large onions, diced**

▲ 6 **carrots, cut in 1-inch slices**

▲ 6 **stalks celery, cut in 1-inch slices**

4 **cloves garlic, sliced**

1 **tablespoon minced fresh thyme**

2 **teaspoons pepper**

▲ 8 **cups reduced-sodium vegetable broth**

▲ 2 **(10-ounce) bags frozen green peas, thawed**

2 **thin slices pumpernickel bread, toasted and cut into cubes**

1 Combine split peas, onions, carrots, celery, garlic, thyme, pepper, and broth in 6-quart slow cooker. Cover and cook until peas are tender, 4–5 hours on high or 8–10 hours on low.

2 About 10 minutes before serving, stir in green peas. Reserve half of stew (about 6 cups) in airtight container and let cool. Cover and refrigerate up to 4 days or freeze up to 3 months.

3 Ladle remaining 6 cups soup evenly into 4 bowls; sprinkle evenly with croutons.

Per serving (about 1½ cups soup and ¼ cup croutons): 300 Cal, 2 g Total Fat, 0 g Sat Fat, 0 g Trans Fat, 0 mg Chol, 280 mg Sod, 56 g Carb, 11 g Sugar, 22 g Fib, 16 g Prot, 87 mg Calc.

6 PointsPlus® value

SECOND TIME AROUND
If frozen, thaw the reserved soup in the refrigerator overnight. Transfer the soup to a medium saucepan. Cover and cook over medium heat, stirring occasionally, until heated through, 8–10 minutes. Add a few tablespoons of water, if needed. Toast 2 thin slices pumpernickel bread and cut into cubes. Divide the stew among 4 bowls; sprinkle evenly with the croutons.

Mexican Bean and Hominy Stew Serves 4 plus leftovers

▲1 cup dried black beans, picked over, rinsed, and drained

▲8 cups reduced-sodium vegetable broth

2 (6-ounce) cans tomato paste

▲1 large sweet onion, quartered

4 cloves garlic, peeled

2 tablespoons dried oregano

▲4 poblano peppers, chopped

▲2 large red onions, sliced

▲1 (15 1/2-ounce) can hominy, rinsed and drained

2 tablespoons ground cumin

1/2 cup chopped fresh cilantro

1/4 cup lime juice

1 Combine beans and enough water to cover by 1 inch in medium saucepan. Bring to boil over medium-high heat. Reduce heat and cook beans 10 minutes. Drain and place in 6-quart slow cooker.

2 Puree 1 cup broth, tomato paste, sweet onion, garlic, and oregano in blender or food processor, in batches if necessary. Transfer to slow cooker. Stir in remaining 7 cups broth, peppers, red onions, hominy, and cumin. Cover and cook until beans are tender, 4–5 hours on high or 8–10 hours on low.

3 Stir in cilantro and lime juice. Reserve half of stew (about 6 2/3 cups) in airtight container and let cool. Cover and refrigerate up to 4 days or freeze up to 3 months.

4 Ladle remaining 6 2/3 cups stew evenly into 4 bowls.

Per serving (about 1 2/3 cups): 231 Cal, 2 g Total Fat, 0 g Sat Fat, 0 g Trans Fat, 0 mg Chol, 604 mg Sod, 46 g Carb, 12 g Sugar, 13 g Fib, 10 g Prot, 107 mg Calc.

SECOND TIME AROUND
If frozen, thaw the reserved stew in the refrigerator overnight. Transfer to a medium saucepan. Cover and cook over medium heat, stirring occasionally, until heated through, 8–10 minutes. Divide the stew among 4 bowls.

Finish With: Melon with Ginger-Lime Syrup, page 131

**Mexican Bean and
Hominy Stew**

Herbed Mushroom-Vegetable Stew with Polenta Serves 4 plus leftovers

▲ 8 ounces cremini mushrooms, left whole

▲ 8 ounces portobello mushrooms, stems discarded, caps sliced

▲ 3 stalks celery, chopped

▲ 1 pound small red potatoes, left whole

▲ 1 small kabocha squash (about 2 pounds), seeded and cut into 1/2-inch chunks

6 cloves garlic, minced

4 tablespoons chopped fresh sage

2 tablespoons chopped fresh thyme

1 teaspoon salt

6 cups water

▲ 1 1/2 cups instant polenta

1 Combine mushrooms, celery, potatoes, squash, garlic, sage, thyme, and salt in a 6-quart slow cooker. Add water and stir to mix well. Cover and cook until vegetables are tender, 3–4 hours on high or 6–8 hours or on low.

2 About 15 minutes before serving, prepare polenta according to package directions.

3 Reserve half of stew (about 6 cups) and half of polenta (about 2 cups) in separate airtight containers and let cool. Cover and refrigerate up to 4 days.

4 Divide remaining 2 cups polenta evenly among 4 bowls; top evenly with remaining 6 cups stew.

Per serving (about 1 1/2 cups stew and 1/2 cup polenta):
233 Cal, 3 g Total Fat, 1 g Sat Fat, 0 g Trans Fat, 0 mg Chol, 605 mg Sod, 46 g Carb, 7 g Sugar, 5 g Fib, 8 g Prot, 108 mg Calc.

6 PointsPlus value

SECOND TIME AROUND

Transfer the reserved stew to a medium saucepan. Cover and cook over medium heat, stirring occasionally, until heated through, 8–10 minutes. Add a few tablespoons of water, if needed. Transfer reserved polenta to a microwavable dish, cover with wax paper, and microwave on High until heated through, 4–5 minutes. Divide the polenta among 4 bowls; top evenly with the stew.

Finish With: Peppered Strawberries with Yogurt, page 131

Greek Eggplant and Sweet Potato Stew Serves 4 plus leftovers

2 tablespoons ground ginger

1 tablespoon cinnamon

2 teaspoons ground allspice

1 teaspoon salt

1/2 teaspoon cayenne

▲ 3 red or yellow bell peppers, cut into 1/2-inch slices

▲ 2 large sweet potatoes (about 2 1/2 pounds), peeled and cut into 1/2-inch rounds

▲ 1 large eggplant, cut into 1/2-inch rounds

▲ 1 large onion, cut into 1/2-inch rounds

1 cup dry white wine

1 (6-ounce) can tomato paste

4 tablespoons crumbled reduced-fat feta cheese

4 tablespoons chopped fresh flat-leaf parsley

1 Stir together ginger, cinnamon, allspice, salt, and cayenne in small bowl.

2 Layer bell peppers, sweet potatoes, eggplant, and onion in 6-quart slow cooker, sprinkling spice mixture between each layer.

3 Whisk together wine and tomato paste in medium bowl; add to slow cooker. Cover and cook until vegetables are tender, 6–8 hours on low.

4 Reserve half of stew (4 cups) in airtight container and let cool. Cover and refrigerate up to 4 days or freeze up to 3 months.

5 Ladle remaining 4 cups stew evenly into 4 bowls; sprinkle evenly with feta and parsley.

Per serving (about 1 cup): 140 Cal, 1 g Total Fat, 0 g Sat Fat, 0 g Trans Fat, 1 mg Chol, 542 mg Sod, 25 g Carb, 10 g Sugar, 9 g Fib, 5 g Prot, 66 mg Calc.

SECOND TIME AROUND

If frozen, thaw the reserved stew in the refrigerator overnight. Transfer to a medium saucepan. Cover and cook over medium heat, stirring occasionally, until heated through, 8–10 minutes. Add a few tablespoons of water, if needed. Divide the stew among 4 bowls; sprinkle evenly with 4 tablespoons crumbled reduced-fat feta cheese and 4 tablespoons chopped fresh flat-leaf parsley.

Make-Ahead
Sweets

Ever wish you could treat yourself and your family to homemade sweets like waffles, scones, muffins, cakes, and cookies, but you just don't have time to prepare them? With these completely make-ahead recipes, you can have a stash of goodies on hand when you need a ready-to-serve breakfast, snack, or even a special occasion dessert.

Whole Wheat Yeast Waffles Serves 8

½ cup warm water

1 teaspoon brown sugar

1 package quick-rise yeast

2 cups warm low-fat (1%) milk (105–115°F)

2 cups white whole wheat flour or all-purpose flour

1 tablespoon unsalted butter, melted

½ teaspoon salt

▲ 2 large egg whites

1 Combine water and brown sugar in large mixing bowl; sprinkle in yeast and let stand until foamy, about 5 minutes.

2 Add milk, flour, butter, and salt to yeast in bowl; whisk until smooth. Cover and refrigerate overnight.

3 Preheat waffle baker according to manufacturer's directions.

4 With electric mixer on high speed, beat egg whites in medium bowl until soft peaks form, about 2 minutes. Gently fold beaten whites into batter until no streaks of white remain.

5 When waffle baker is ready, spray baker with nonstick spray. Pour batter onto center and quickly spread to within 1 inch of edges. Close baker and bake as manufacturer directs; do not open until done. Repeat, reheating waffle baker and spraying with nonstick spray before adding each batch of batter.

Per serving (2 waffles): 149 Cal, 3 g Total Fat, 1 g Sat Fat, 0 g Trans Fat, 7 mg Chol, 189 mg Sod, 26 g Carb, 4 g Sugar, 4 g Fib, 7 g Prot, 85 mg Calc.

STORE AND SERVE LATER

Place the waffles on a wire rack and let cool completely. Place in heavy zip-close plastic bags and freeze up to 3 months. To reheat, toast waffles in toaster until crisp, about 2 minutes.

Cranberry-Pumpkin Scones Serves 12

2¹/₂ cups white whole wheat flour or all purpose flour

¹/₄ cup packed brown sugar

2 teaspoons baking powder

¹/₂ teaspoon salt

1 teaspoon ground ginger

3 tablespoons cold unsalted butter, cut into small pieces

▲ 1 cup canned pumpkin

▲ 1 large egg, lightly beaten

¹/₂ cup dried cranberries

¹/₄ cup plus 1 tablespoon low-fat (1%) milk

1 tablespoon raw (turbinado) sugar

1 Preheat oven to 400°F. Line large baking sheet with parchment paper.

2 Combine flour, brown sugar, baking powder, salt, and ginger in large bowl. With pastry blender, cut in butter until mixture is crumbly. Add pumpkin, egg, cranberries, and ¹/₄ cup milk and stir just until moistened.

3 Sprinkle work surface lightly with flour. Turn dough onto surface and knead lightly. Divide dough in half and pat each piece into 6-inch round. Cut each round into 6 wedges. Transfer wedges to prepared baking sheet. Brush scones with remaining 1 tablespoon milk; sprinkle evenly with raw sugar.

4 Bake until toothpick inserted into centers comes out clean, 18 minutes. Transfer scones to wire rack and let cool 5 minutes. Serve warm.

Per serving (1 scone): 164 Cal, 4 g Total Fat, 2 g Sat Fat, 0 g Trans Fat, 26 mg Chol, 201 mg Sod, 30 g Carb, 10 g Sugar, 4 g Fib, 4 g Prot, 44 mg Calc.

STORE AND SERVE LATER

Let the scones cool completely on a wire rack. Place in heavy zip-close plastic bags and freeze up to 3 months. To reheat, place one scone on a microwavable plate, cover with wax paper, and microwave on High until heated through, about 30 seconds.

Cottage Cheese Waffles with Raspberries Serves 8 🕐

1 cup reduced-fat (2%) cottage cheese

2 cups low-fat (1%) milk

▲ ¼ cup fat-free egg substitute

1 tablespoon brown sugar

1 teaspoon grated lemon zest

1 teaspoon grated orange zest

1 teaspoon vanilla extract

2 cups white whole wheat flour or all purpose flour

2 teaspoons baking powder

¼ teaspoon salt

▲ 2¾ cups fresh raspberries

2 teaspoons confectioners' sugar

1 Preheat waffle baker according to manufacturer's directions.

2 Puree cottage cheese in food processor or blender. Add milk, egg substitute, brown sugar, lemon zest, orange zest, and vanilla and pulse until well blended. Add flour, baking powder, and salt and pulse until well blended.

3 When waffle baker is ready, spray baker with nonstick spray. Pour batter onto center and quickly spread to within 1 inch of edges. Close baker and bake as manufacturer directs; do not open until done. Repeat, reheating waffle baker and spraying with nonstick spray before adding each batch of batter. Top with raspberries and sprinkle with confectioners' sugar just before serving.

Per serving (2 waffles and ⅓ cup raspberries): 187 Cal, 2 g Total Fat, 1 g Sat Fat, 0 g Trans Fat, 6 mg Chol, 343 mg Sod, 33 g Carb, 8 g Sugar, 6 g Fib, 10 g Prot, 152 mg Calc.

5 PointsPlus® value

STORE AND SERVE LATER

Place the waffles on a wire rack and let cool completely. Place in heavy zip-close plastic bags and freeze up to 3 months. To reheat, toast waffles in toaster until crisp, about 2 minutes. Top with raspberries and sprinkle with confectioners' sugar just before serving.

**Cottage Cheese Waffles
with Raspberries**

Ginger-Date Muffins Serves 12

2½ cups white whole wheat
flour or all-purpose flour

2 teaspoons baking
powder

1½ teaspoons ground
ginger

½ teaspoon ground
allspice

1 teaspoon baking soda

½ teaspoon salt

1½ cups low-fat buttermilk

½ cup packed dark brown
sugar

¼ cup canola oil

▲ 2 large eggs

1 teaspoon vanilla extract

1 cup pitted dates,
chopped

1 Preheat oven to 400°F. Line 12 muffin cups with paper liners; spray liners with nonstick spray.

2 Combine flour, baking powder, ginger, allspice, baking soda, and salt in large bowl. Whisk together buttermilk, brown sugar, oil, eggs, and vanilla in medium bowl. Add buttermilk mixture and dates to flour mixture and stir just until blended.

3 Fill muffin cups evenly with batter. Bake until golden brown and toothpick inserted into centers of muffins comes out clean, 15 minutes. Cool in pan on wire rack 5 minutes. Remove muffins from pan and cool on rack. Serve warm or at room temperature.

Per serving (1 muffin): 244 Cal, 6 g Total Fat, 1 g Sat Fat, 0 g Trans Fat, 37 mg Chol, 242 mg Sod, 42 g Carb, 20 g Sugar, 4 g Fib, 6 g Prot, 70 mg Calc.

STORE AND SERVE LATER
Let the muffins cool completely on a wire rack. Place in heavy zip-close plastic bags and freeze up to 3 months. To reheat, place one muffin on a microwavable plate, cover with wax paper, and microwave on High until heated through, about 30 seconds.

Banana-Oat-Coconut Muffins Serves 12

2¹/₄ cups white whole wheat flour or all-purpose flour

1¹/₂ cups old-fashioned oats

³/₄ cup shredded unsweetened coconut

2 teaspoons baking soda

1 teaspoon ground nutmeg

¹/₂ teaspoon salt

▲ 3 large ripe bananas, mashed

1¹/₂ cups low-fat buttermilk

¹/₃ cup packed light brown sugar

▲ 3 large egg whites

3 tablespoons canola oil

1 Preheat oven to 400°F. Line 12 muffin cups with paper liners; spray liners with nonstick spray.

2 Combine flour, oats, coconut, baking soda, nutmeg, and salt in large bowl. Whisk together bananas, buttermilk, brown sugar, egg whites, and oil in another large bowl. Add banana mixture to flour mixture and stir just until blended.

3 Fill muffin cups evenly with batter. Bake until golden brown and toothpick inserted into centers comes out clean, 18 minutes.

4 Cool in pan on wire rack 5 minutes. Remove muffins from pan and cool on rack. Serve warm or at room temperature.

Per serving (1 muffin): 269 Cal, 9 g Total Fat, 4 g Sat Fat, 0 g Trans Fat, 1 mg Chol, 356 mg Sod, 41 g Carb, 12 g Sugar, 6 g Fib, 7 g Prot, 43 mg Calc.

STORE AND SERVE LATER

Let the muffins cool completely on a wire rack. Place in heavy zip-close plastic bags and freeze up to 3 months. To reheat, place one muffin on a microwavable plate, cover with wax paper, and microwave on High until heated through, about 30 seconds.

**Raisin-Oat Scones and Glazed
Honey-Peach Mini Muffins, 132**

Raisin-Oat Scones Serves 10

1¼ cups old-fashioned oats

1 cup white whole wheat flour or all-purpose flour

3 tablespoons brown sugar

2 teaspoons baking powder

½ teaspoon salt

3 tablespoons cold unsalted butter, cut into small pieces

½ cup low-fat buttermilk

▲ 1 large egg

1 teaspoon vanilla extract

½ cup golden raisins

1 Preheat oven to 400°F.

2 Combine 1 cup oats, flour, brown sugar, baking powder, and salt in large bowl. With pastry blender, cut in butter until mixture is crumbly.

3 Whisk together buttermilk, egg, and vanilla in small bowl. Add buttermilk mixture and raisins to oat mixture, stirring until moistened.

4 Sprinkle work surface with remaining ¼ cup oats; transfer dough to work surface and turn to coat with oats. Pat dough into an 8-inch round (dough will be sticky). Cut into 10 wedges; transfer wedges to ungreased baking sheet.

5 Bake until toothpick inserted into centers comes out clean, 15 minutes. Transfer scones to wire rack and let cool 5 minutes. Serve warm.

Per serving (1 scone): 173 Cal, 5 g Total Fat, 2 g Sat Fat, 0 g Trans Fat, 31 mg Chol, 250 mg Sod, 28 g Carb, 10 g Sugar, 3 g Fib, 4 g Prot, 45 mg Calc.

STORE AND SERVE LATER

Let the scones cool completely on a wire rack. Place in heavy zip-close plastic bags and freeze up to 3 months. To reheat, place one scone on a microwavable plate, cover with wax paper, and microwave on High until heated through, about 30 seconds.

Quick Fruit Desserts to Serve 4

2 PointsPlus® value
PER SERVING

Microwave Baked Apples

Halve and core **4 small Rome apples**; place cut side up in large microwavable dish. Stir together **2 tablespoons apple juice or orange juice**, **1 tablespoon light brown sugar**, and **¼ teaspoon ground cinnamon** in small bowl; pour over apples. Cover with wax paper and microwave on High until apples are tender, 5–7 minutes. Let stand 2 minutes. Serve apples with cooking juices.

2 PointsPlus® value
PER SERVING

Nectarines with Raspberry-Yogurt Sauce

Pit and slice **4 nectarines** and divide evenly among 4 bowls. Whisk together **⅓ cup plain low-fat Greek yogurt** and **1 tablespoon seedless raspberry jam** in small bowl. Spoon evenly over nectarines.

3 PointsPlus® value
PER SERVING

Honeyed Fruits with Toasted Almonds

Whisk together **1 teaspoon grated lemon zest**, **2 tablespoons lemon juice**, and **1 tablespoon honey** in large bowl. Add **2 apples, cored and sliced**, **2 cups seedless grapes**, and **2 tablespoons sliced almonds**, toasted, and toss to coat.

3 PointsPlus® value
PER SERVING

Maple-Mint Fruit Compote

Stir together **2 tablespoons maple syrup**, **2 tablespoons lime juice**, and **1 tablespoon minced fresh mint** in large bowl. Add **1 cup pineapple chunks**, **1 cup seedless grapes**, **½ cup fresh blueberries**, and **1 kiwifruit, peeled and sliced**, and toss to coat.

Molasses-Spice Roasted Pears

3 PER SERVING

Preheat oven to 400°F; spray large baking pan with nonstick spray. Halve and core **4 pears;** arrange cut side down in baking pan. Bake until pears are tender, about 20 minutes. Whisk together **3 tablespoons apple juice or orange juice, 1 tablespoon molasses,** and **⅛ teaspoon nutmeg;** pour over pears. Bake 5 minutes longer. Serve pears with cooking juices.

Orange-Glazed Tropical Fruits

3 PER SERVING

Stir together **3 tablespoons orange juice** and **2 tablespoons orange marmalade** in large bowl. Add **2 kiwifruits, peeled and sliced, 1 banana, peeled and sliced,** and **1 mango, peeled, pitted and sliced,** and toss to coat.

Peppered Strawberries with Yogurt

3 PER SERVING

Toss together **2 cups hulled strawberries, 1 tablespoon light brown sugar, ⅛ teaspoon freshly ground black pepper,** and **½ teaspoon lemon juice** in medium bowl; let stand, stirring occasionally, 10 minutes. Whisk together **2 cups fat-free plain Greek yogurt** and **1 tablespoon light brown sugar.** Divide yogurt mixture evenly among 4 bowls; top evenly with strawberry mixture.

Browned Butter Pineapple Sundaes

4 PER SERVING

Melt **1 tablespoon butter** in large nonstick skillet over medium-high heat; cook until butter is lightly browned, about 1 minute. Add **2 cups fresh pineapple chunks** and **1 tablespoon light brown sugar.** Cook, stirring constantly, until pineapple is lightly browned, about 2 minutes. Place **¼-cup scoop light vanilla ice cream** in each of 4 bowls; top evenly with pineapple mixture.

Melon with Ginger-Lime Syrup

4 PER SERVING

Combine **¼ cup lime juice** and **2 tablespoons sugar** in small saucepan; set over medium heat and cook, stirring until sugar dissolves. Transfer to small bowl; stir in **1 teaspoon grated peeled fresh ginger** and cool to room temperature. Arrange **½ honeydew** and **½ cantaloupe,** peeled and sliced on platter; drizzle with syrup.

Rum and Coconut Bananas

5 PER SERVING

Cook **2 tablespoons light brown sugar, 2 tablespoons dark rum,** and **¼ teaspoon ground cinnamon** in large nonstick skillet over medium heat, stirring constantly, until sugar melts. Add **4 small bananas, cut lengthwise in half, then crosswise in half;** cook, stirring constantly, until bananas are lightly browned. Stir in **1 tablespoon butter** until melted. Sprinkle with **2 tablespoons sweetened flaked coconut.**

Glazed Honey-Peach Mini Muffins Makes 48

1½ cups all-purpose flour

1 cup whole wheat flour

2 teaspoons baking powder

1 teaspoon baking soda

½ teaspoon salt

1½ cups low-fat buttermilk

▲ ¼ cup fat-free egg substitute

¼ cup honey

¼ cup unsalted butter, melted and cooled

1 tablespoon vanilla extract

▲ 1½ cups peeled diced peaches

1 cup confectioners' sugar

4 teaspoons low-fat (1%) milk

1 Preheat oven to 400°F. Line 48 mini-muffin cups with paper liners; spray liners with nonstick spray

2 Combine all-purpose and whole wheat flours, baking powder, baking soda, and salt in large bowl. Whisk together buttermilk, egg substitute, honey, butter, and vanilla in medium bowl. Add buttermilk mixture and peaches to flour mixture and stir until moistened.

3 Fill muffin cups evenly with batter. Bake until browned and toothpick inserted into centers comes out clean, about 15 minutes.

4 Cool in pan on wire rack 5 minutes. Remove muffins from pan and cool on rack.

5 To make glaze, combine confectioners' sugar and milk in small bowl; stir until smooth. Drizzle glaze over muffins.

Per serving (2 muffins): 106 Cal, 2 g Total Fat, 1 g Sat Fat, 0 g Trans Fat, 6 mg Chol, 92 mg Sod, 19 g Carb, 9 g Sugar, 1 g Fib, 2 g Prot, 28 mg Calc.

STORE AND SERVE LATER
Place the unglazed muffins in heavy zip-close plastic bags and freeze up to 3 months. To serve, thaw at room temperature overnight. Drizzle with glaze just before serving.

Apple-Fig Muffins Serves 12

1³/₄ cups white whole wheat flour or all-purpose flour

1 teaspoon baking powder

1 teaspoon baking soda

¹/₂ teaspoon salt

¹/₂ teaspoon ground cinnamon

▲ 1 cup unsweetened applesauce

³/₄ cup low-fat buttermilk

4 tablespoons honey

3 tablespoons unsalted butter, melted and cooled

▲ 2 large eggs

1 cup chopped dried figs

1 Preheat oven to 400°F. Line 12 muffin cups with paper liners; spray liners with nonstick spray.

2 Combine flour, baking powder, baking soda, salt, and cinnamon in large bowl. Whisk together applesauce, buttermilk, 3 tablespoons honey, butter, and eggs in medium bowl. Add applesauce mixture and figs to flour mixture and stir just until blended.

3 Fill muffin cups evenly with batter. Bake until golden brown and toothpick inserted into centers comes out clean, 18 minutes. Brush tops of hot muffins with remaining 1 table-spoon honey. Cool in pan on wire rack 5 minutes. Remove muffins from pan and cool on rack. Serve warm or at room temperature.

Per serving (1 muffin): 175 Cal, 4 g Total Fat, 2 g Sat Fat, 0 g Trans Fat, 44 mg Chol, 277 mg Sod, 31 g Carb, 14 g Sugar, 4 g Fib, 4 g Prot, 53 mg Calc.

4 PointsPlus® value

STORE AND SERVE LATER

Let the muffins cool completely on a wire rack. Place in heavy zip-close plastic bags and freeze up to 3 months. To reheat, place one muffin on a microwavable plate, cover with wax paper, and microwave on High until heated through, about 30 seconds.

Orange-Rosemary Semolina Cake with Strawberries Serves 12

1½ cups **water**

¼ cup **fine semolina (durum wheat) flour**

6 tablespoons **granulated sugar**

1 **(15-ounce) container part-skim ricotta cheese**

▲ 2 large **eggs, separated**

2 tablespoons **orange-flavored liqueur**

2 teaspoons **chopped fresh rosemary**

1 teaspoon **grated orange zest**

¼ teaspoon **salt**

1 teaspoon **confectioners' sugar**

▲ 4 cups **sliced strawberries**

1 Preheat oven to 350°F. Spray 9 x 1½-inch inch cake pan or springform pan with nonstick spray.

2 Bring water to boil in small saucepan over medium-high heat. Slowly pour in semolina flour in thin steady stream, whisking constantly. Add 4 tablespoons granulated sugar, and cook, stirring constantly, until thickened, 4 minutes. Transfer to bowl and let cool slightly.

3 Whisk together ricotta, egg yolks, liqueur, rosemary, and orange zest in large bowl. Stir in semolina mixture.

4 With electric mixer at medium speed, beat egg whites and salt until frothy. Slowly add remaining 2 tablespoons sugar, beating until stiff glossy peaks form. With rubber spatula, gently fold beaten egg white mixture into ricotta mixture until no streaks of white remain.

5 Spoon into prepared pan. Bake until puffed and golden, 1 hour. Let cool on wire rack 10 minutes. Run thin knife around edge of cake to loosen from pan. Invert onto serving plate; lift off pan. Let cool completely. Serve at room temperature. Sprinkle with confectioners' sugar just before serving. Serve with strawberries.

Per serving (¹⁄₁₂ of cake with ¹⁄₃ cup strawberries): 115 Cal, 4 g Total Fat, 2g Sat Fat, 0 g Trans Fat, 47 mg Chol, 105 mg Sod, 15 g Carb, 9 g Sugar, 1 g Fib, 6 g Prot, 111 mg Calc.

STORE AND SERVE LATER

Tightly wrap the cake in plastic wrap and then in heavy-duty foil and freeze up to 3 months. To serve, thaw at room temperature overnight. Sprinkle with 1 teaspoon confectioners' sugar just before serving and top with strawberries.

**Orange-Rosemary Semolina
Cake with Strawberries**

Peppery Pear Gingerbread Serves 16

1   tablespoon plus ⅓ cup unsalted butter, softened

▲ 1   large pear, peeled, cored, and thinly sliced

1¼ cups all-purpose flour

1   cup white whole wheat flour

1½ teaspoons baking soda

½   teaspoon salt

½   teaspoon freshly ground black pepper

½   teaspoon ground ginger

½   cup packed dark brown sugar

¼   cup unsulphured molasses

▲ ¼   cup fat-free egg substitute

1   tablespoon grated peeled fresh ginger

1   cup low-fat buttermilk

▲ 2   cups plain fat-free yogurt

1   Preheat oven to 350°F. Coat 9-inch round cake pan with nonstick spray.

2   Heat 1 tablespoon butter in large heavy skillet over medium-high heat. Add pear and cook, stirring often, until softened and lightly browned, about 5 minutes. Transfer to small bowl and let cool.

3   Whisk together flours, baking soda, salt, pepper, and ground ginger in large bowl.

4   With electric mixer on medium speed, beat brown sugar and remaining ⅓ cup butter until light and fluffy, about 3 minutes. Beat in molasses, egg substitute, and fresh ginger. Reduce mixer speed to low. Beat in flour mixture alternately with buttermilk, beginning and ending with flour mixture, beating just until blended. Gently stir in pears. Spoon batter into prepared pan. Bake until toothpick inserted into center comes out clean, about 35 minutes.

5   Let cool on wire rack 15 minutes. Remove from pan and let cool on wire rack. Serve warm or at room temperature. Serve with yogurt.

Per serving (¹⁄₁₆ of cake and 2 tablespoons yogurt): 180 Cal, 5 g Total Fat, 3 g Sat Fat, 0 g Trans Fat, 13 mg Chol, 241 mg Sod, 29 g Carb, 14 g Sugar, 2 g Fib, 5 g Prot, 100 mg Calc.

STORE AND SERVE LATER

Tightly wrap the gingerbread in plastic wrap and then in heavy-duty foil and freeze up to 3 months. To serve, thaw at room temperature overnight. Serve with yogurt.

Carrot-Ginger Chiffon Cake Serves 12

1½ cups carrot juice

1½ cups cake flour

1 tablespoon baking powder

½ teaspoon salt

1 teaspoon ground ginger

1¼ cups sugar

▲ 7 large eggs separated, at room temperature

¼ cup canola oil

¼ teaspoon cream of tartar

1½ tablespoons confectioners' sugar

1 Place an oven rack in lower third of oven and preheat oven to 325°F.

2 Cook carrot juice in small saucepan over medium-high heat until reduced by half, about 10 minutes. Transfer to small bowl and let cool.

3 Sift together flour, baking powder, salt, and ginger in large bowl; stir in 1 cup sugar. Place egg yolks in another large bowl and whisk until pale and thickened. Whisk in carrot juice, then whisk in oil in slow steady stream. Add egg yolk mixture to flour mixture and whisk until smooth.

4 With electric mixer on medium speed, beat egg whites and cream of tartar in large bowl until frothy. Increase speed to high. Beat in remaining ¼ cup sugar, one tablespoon at a time, beating until stiff glossy peaks form. Gently fold beaten whites into batter until no streaks of white remain.

5 Pour batter into ungreased 10-inch tube pan; smooth top of batter. Bake until top of cake springs back when lightly pressed, 1 hour.

6 Invert tube pan onto bottleneck or inverted metal funnel and cool completely. To loosen cake, run knife around sides of pan and center tube. Unmold cake onto serving plate. Sprinkle with confectioners' sugar just before serving.

Per serving (¹⁄₁₂ of cake): 217 Cal, 7 g Total Fat, 1 g Sat Fat, 0 g Trans Fat, 125 mg Chol, 293 mg Sod, 34 g Carb, 16 g Sugar, 0 g Fib, 5 g Prot, 44 mg Calc.

STORE AND SERVE LATER
Tightly wrap the cake in plastic wrap and then in heavy-duty foil and freeze up to 3 months. To serve, thaw at room temperature overnight. Sprinkle with 1½ tablespoons confectioners' sugar just before serving.

Earl Grey Apple-Cherry Cake

Earl Grey Apple-Cherry Cake Serves 16

1½ cups dried apples, chopped

1 cup dried sour cherries

1 Earl Grey tea bag

1 cup water

1 cup packed light brown sugar

¼ cup all-fruit orange marmalade

▲ 1 large egg

1 teaspoon grated lemon zest

1½ cups all-purpose flour

1 cup white whole wheat flour or all-purpose flour

1 teaspoon cinnamon

½ teaspoon ground nutmeg

½ teaspoon baking soda

¼ teaspoon salt

1 teaspoon confectioners' sugar

1 Combine apples, cherries, and tea bag in large bowl. Bring water to boil in small saucepan; pour water over apple mixture. Cover and let stand 1 hour. Remove and discard tea bag.

2 Preheat oven to 350°F. Spray 9-inch Bundt pan with nonstick spray.

3 Add brown sugar, marmalade, egg, and lemon zest to apple mixture; stir until well combined. Whisk together flours, cinnamon, nutmeg, baking soda, and salt in medium bowl; add to apple mixture and stir just until blended.

4 Spoon batter into prepared pan. Bake until toothpick inserted into center comes out clean, about 45 minutes. Cool completely in pan on wire rack. Remove from pan. Sprinkle with confectioners' sugar just before serving.

Per serving (¹⁄₁₆ of cake): 189 Cal, 1 g Total Fat, 0 g Sat Fat, 0 g Trans Fat, 13 mg Chol, 135 mg Sod, 43 g Carb, 23 g Sugar, 4 g Fib, 3 g Prot, 21 mg Calc.

STORE AND SERVE LATER

Tightly wrap the cake in plastic wrap and then in heavy-duty foil and freeze up to 3 months. To serve, thaw at room temperature overnight. Sprinkle with 1 teaspoon confectioners' sugar just before serving.

Margarita Chiffon Cupcakes Makes 24

1½ cups cake flour

1 tablespoon baking powder

½ teaspoon salt

1¼ cups granulated sugar

▲ 7 large eggs separated, at room temperature

2 teaspoons grated lime zest

¼ cup lime juice

¼ cup orange juice

3 tablespoons orange-flavored liqueur

¼ cup canola oil

¼ teaspoon cream of tartar

1½ tablespoons confectioners' sugar

1 Preheat oven to 325°F. Line 24 muffin cups with paper liners; spray liners with nonstick spray.

2 Sift together cake flour, baking powder, and salt in large bowl. Stir in 1 cup sugar.

3 Whisk egg yolks in medium bowl until pale and thickened. Whisk in lime zest, lime juice, orange juice, and liqueur. Add oil in slow steady stream, whisking constantly. Add egg yolk mixture to flour mixture and whisk until smooth.

4 With mixer on medium speed, beat egg whites and cream of tartar in large bowl until soft peaks form. Increase speed to high. Add remaining ¼ cup granulated sugar, one tablespoon at a time, beating until stiff peaks form. With rubber spatula, fold one-fourth of beaten whites into batter. Gently fold in remaining whites just until no streaks of white remain.

5 Spoon batter into prepared muffin cups. Bake until toothpick inserted into centers comes out clean, about 25 minutes.

6 Let cool in pans on wire racks 10 minutes; remove cupcakes from pans and let cool completely on racks. Sprinkle with confectioners' sugar just before serving.

Per serving (1 cupcake): 115 Cal, 4 g Total Fat, 1 g Sat Fat, 0 g Trans Fat, 63 mg Chol, 137 mg Sod, 18 g Carb, 9 g Sugar, 0 g Fib, 2 g Prot, 20 mg Calc.

STORE AND SERVE LATER

Place the cupcakes in heavy zip-close plastic bags and freeze up to 3 months. To serve, thaw at room temperature overnight. Sprinkle with 1½ tablespoons confectioners' sugar just before serving.

Strawberry-Almond Cupcakes Serves 12

1/4 cup sliced almonds

1/2 cup granulated sugar

1 cup all-purpose flour

1/2 teaspoon baking powder

1/2 teaspoon baking soda

1/4 teaspoon salt

1/2 cup low-fat (1%) milk

4 tablespoons unsalted butter, melted and cooled

▲ 1 large egg

1 teaspoon almond extract

1/4 cup strawberry fruit spread

2 teaspoons confectioners' sugar

1 Preheat oven to 350°F.

2 Spread almonds on small baking sheet. Bake, stirring once, until toasted, 8–10 minutes. Transfer to plate to cool.

3 Maintain oven temperature. Line 12 muffin cups with paper liners; spray liners with nonstick spray.

4 Combine almonds and 1/4 cup granulated sugar in food processor and pulse until almonds are finely ground.

5 Whisk together flour, baking powder, baking soda, and salt in large bowl. Whisk together milk, butter, egg, almond extract, and remaining 1/4 cup granulated sugar in medium bowl. Add milk mixture to flour mixture and whisk until smooth. Gently stir in almond mixture.

6 Spoon batter evenly into muffin cups. Top each with 1 teaspoon of fruit spread. Swirl with knife to create marbled effect. Bake until toothpick inserted into center comes out clean, 15–17 minutes.

7 Let cool in pans on wire racks 10 minutes; remove cupcakes from pans and let cool completely on racks. Sprinkle with confectioners' sugar just before serving.

Per serving (1 cupcake): 129 Cal, 5 g Total Fat, 3 g Sat Fat, 0 g Trans Fat, 29 mg Chol, 134 mg Sod, 19 g Carb, 10 g Sugar, 1 g Fib, 2 g Prot, 26 mg Calc.

STORE AND SERVE LATER

Place the cupcakes in heavy zip-close plastic bags and freeze up to 3 months. To serve, thaw at room temperature overnight. Sprinkle with 2 teaspoons confectioners' sugar just before serving.

Mini–Chocolate Cheesecakes Serves 6

8	chocolate wafer cookies, crumbled
1	(15-ounce) container low-fat ricotta cheese
1/2	cup sugar
▲ 1	large egg
▲ 1	large egg white
1/4	cup unsweetened cocoa
1	teaspoon vanilla extract
▲ 1 1/2	cups fresh raspberries

1 Preheat oven to 300°F. Spray 6 (6-ounce) ramekins with nonstick cooking spray.

2 Pulse cookies in food processor until finely ground. Divide crumbs evenly among ramekins. Wipe out food processor.

3 Puree ricotta and sugar in food processor. Add egg, egg white, cocoa, and vanilla and pulse until well mixed. Spoon batter evenly into prepared ramekins. Place ramekins in large baking pan. Put pan in oven and add enough hot water to pan to come 1 inch up side of custard cups.

4 Bake until cheesecakes are set, about 40 minutes. Remove pan from oven and let cheesecakes stand 5 minutes. Carefully remove from water bath; let cool completely. Cover and refrigerate until chilled, at least 4 hours. Serve with raspberries.

Per serving (1 cheesecake and 1/4 cup raspberries): 184 Cal, 5 g Total Fat, 3 g Sat Fat, 0 g Trans Fat, 53 mg Chol, 130 mg Sod, 27 g Carb, 19 g Sugar, 3 g Fib, 9 g Prot, 133 mg Calc.

STORE AND SERVE LATER
Tightly wrap the cheesecakes in plastic wrap. If freezing, then wrap in heavy-duty foil. Refrigerate up to 3 days or freeze up to 3 months. If frozen, thaw in the refrigerator overnight. Bring to room temperature before serving and serve with 1 1/2 cups fresh raspberries.

Mini–Chocolate Cheesecakes

Sour Cream–Chocolate Cupcakes Serves 12

1½ cups all-purpose flour

½ cup plus 1 teaspoon unsweetened cocoa

¾ teaspoon baking soda

½ teaspoon baking powder

¼ teaspoon salt

¾ cup low-fat (1%) milk

½ cup reduced-fat sour cream

½ cup granulated sugar

¼ cup unsalted butter, melted and cooled

▲ ¼ cup fat-free egg substitute

2 teaspoons vanilla extract

1 teaspoon instant espresso powder

1 teaspoon confectioners' sugar

1 Preheat oven to 350°F. Line 12 muffin cups with paper liners; spray liners with nonstick spray.

2 Whisk together flour, ½ cup cocoa, baking soda, baking powder, and salt in large bowl. Whisk together milk, sour cream, granulated sugar, butter, egg substitute, vanilla, and espresso powder in medium bowl. Add milk mixture to flour mixture; whisk until smooth.

3 Spoon batter evenly into muffin cups. Bake until toothpick inserted into centers comes out clean, about 18 minutes.

4 Let cool in pans on wire racks 10 minutes; remove cupcakes from pans and let cool completely on racks. Sprinkle with confectioners' sugar and remaining 1 teaspoon cocoa just before serving.

Per serving (1 cupcake): 150 Cal, 6 g Total Fat, 4 g Sat Fat, 0 g Trans Fat, 15 mg Chol, 173 mg Sod, 22 g Carb, 7 g Sugar, 2 g Fib, 4 g Prot, 47 mg Calc.

STORE AND SERVE LATER
Place the cupcakes in heavy zip-close plastic bags and freeze up to 3 months. To serve, thaw at room temperature overnight. Sprinkle with 1 teaspoon confectioners' sugar and 1 teaspoon unsweetened cocoa just before serving.

French Honey and Spice Cake Serves 16

3 cups white whole wheat flour

2 teaspoons baking soda

1 teaspoon ground cinnamon

1 teaspoon ground ginger

1 teaspoon anise seeds

1/2 teaspoon black pepper

1/2 teaspoon baking powder

1/2 teaspoon salt

1/4 teaspoon ground cloves

1 cup low-fat (1%) milk

1/2 cup orange marmalade

1/3 cup unsalted butter, melted and cooled

1/4 cup packed dark brown sugar

1/4 cup honey

▲ 1 large egg

1 Preheat oven to 350°F. Spray 9 x 5-inch loaf pan with nonstick spray, then dust with flour.

2 Whisk together flour, baking soda, cinnamon, ginger, anise seeds, pepper, baking powder, salt, and cloves in large bowl. Whisk together milk, marmalade, butter, brown sugar, honey, and egg in medium bowl. Add milk mixture to flour mixture and stir until well blended.

3 Spoon batter into prepared pan and bake until toothpick inserted into center comes out clean, about 55 minutes. Let cool in pan on wire rack 10 minutes. Remove from pan and cool completely on rack.

Per serving (1/16 of loaf): 188 Cal, 5 g Total Fat, 3 g Sat Fat, 0 g Trans Fat, 24 mg Chol, 260 mg Sod, 32 g Carb, 13 g Sugar, 3 g Fib, 4 g Prot, 30 mg Calc.

5 PointsPlus® value

STORE AND SERVE LATER
Place the loaf in a heavy zip-close plastic bag and store at room temperature up to 1 week or freeze up to 3 months. If frozen, thaw at room temperature.

Apricot–Poppy Seed Bread

Apricot–Poppy Seed Bread Serves 16

2 1/2 cups white whole
    wheat flour

2   tablespoons poppy
    seeds

2   teaspoons baking
    powder

1   teaspoon baking soda

1/2   teaspoon salt

1 1/4 cups low-fat buttermilk

1/2   cup packed brown sugar

1/3   cup butter, melted
    and cooled

▲ 2   large eggs

2   tablespoons apricot
    brandy or dry sherry

1   tablespoon grated
    lemon zest

1 1/2 cups diced dried
    apricots

1 Preheat oven to 350°F. Spray 9 x 5-inch loaf pan with nonstick spray, then dust with flour.

2 Whisk together flour, poppy seeds, baking powder, baking soda, and salt in large bowl. Whisk together buttermilk, brown sugar, butter, eggs, brandy, and lemon zest in medium bowl. Add buttermilk mixture to flour mixture and stir until well blended. Stir in apricots.

3 Spoon batter into prepared pan. Bake until toothpick inserted into center comes out clean, about 55 minutes. Let cool in pan on wire rack 10 minutes. Remove from pan and cool completely on rack.

Per serving (1/16 of loaf): 192 Cal, 6 g Total Fat, 3 g Sat Fat, 0 g Trans Fat, 38 mg Chol, 252 mg Sod, 31 g Carb, 14 g Sugar, 4 g Fib, 5 g Prot, 68 mg Calc.

STORE AND SERVE LATER
Place the loaf in a heavy zip-close plastic bag and store at room temperature up to 1 week or freeze up to 3 months. If frozen, thaw at room temperature.

Dried Fig and Fennel Bread Serves 16

2 cups bread flour

1/2 cup rye flour

2 tablespoons fennel seed

2 teaspoons baking powder

1 teaspoon baking soda

1/2 teaspoon salt

1 1/2 cups low-fat buttermilk

1/2 cup brown sugar

1/3 cup unsalted butter, melted and cooled

▲ 2 large eggs

1 1/2 cups diced dried Calimyrna or Smyrna figs

1 Preheat oven to 350°F. Spray 9 x 5-inch loaf pan with nonstick spray, then dust with flour.

2 Whisk together bread flour, rye flour, fennel seed, baking powder, baking soda, and salt in large bowl. Whisk together buttermilk, brown sugar, butter, and eggs in medium bowl. Add buttermilk mixture and figs to flour mixture and stir until well blended.

3 Spoon batter into prepared pan. Bake until toothpick inserted into center comes out clean, about 55 minutes. Let cool in pan on wire rack 10 minutes. Remove from pan and cool completely on rack.

Per serving (1/16 of loaf): 190 Cal, 5 g Total Fat, 3 g Sat Fat, 0 g Trans Fat, 38 mg Chol, 257 mg Sod, 33 g Carb, 15 g Sugar, 3 g Fib, 4 g Prot, 83 mg Calc.

STORE AND SERVE LATER

Place the loaf in a heavy zip-close plastic bag and store at room temperature up to 1 week or freeze up to 3 months. If frozen, thaw at room temperature.

Sweet Potato–Thyme Cornbread Serves 18

2 cups white whole wheat flour

2 cups cornmeal

1/3 cup sugar

1 tablespoon baking powder

1/2 teaspoon baking soda

1/2 teaspoon salt

▲ 2 cups mashed cooked sweet potato

1 1/2 cups low-fat sour cream

▲ 1/2 cup fat-free egg substitute

1/2 cup low-fat buttermilk

1/4 cup unsalted butter, melted and cooled

1 tablespoon chopped fresh thyme or 1 teaspoon dried thyme

1 Preheat oven to 375°F. Coat 9 x 13-inch baking pan with nonstick spray.

2 Whisk together flour, cornmeal, sugar, baking powder, baking soda, and salt in large bowl. Whisk together sweet potato, sour cream, egg substitute, buttermilk, butter, and thyme in medium bowl. Add sweet potato mixture to flour mixture and stir until well blended.

3 Spoon into prepared pan and bake until toothpick inserted into center comes out clean, about 35 minutes. Let cool in pan on wire rack 10 minutes. Remove from pan and cool completely on rack. Serve warm or at room temperature.

Per serving (1/18 of loaf): 207 Cal, 6 g Total Fat, 3 g Sat Fat, 0 g Trans Fat, 14 mg Chol, 231 mg Sod, 33 g Carb, 4 g Sugar, 3 g Fib, 5 g Prot, 61 mg Calc.

STORE AND SERVE LATER

Place the loaf in a heavy zip-close plastic bag and store at room temperature up to 2 days or freeze up to 3 months. If frozen, thaw at room temperature.

Jasmine Rice Pudding with Coconut Serves 8

2½ cups water

1 cup jasmine rice

½ teaspoon salt

▲ 1½ cups fat-free milk

1 (15-ounce) can light (reduced-fat) coconut milk

⅓ cup packed brown sugar

1 teaspoon orange flower water or vanilla extract

3 tablespoons shredded unsweetened coconut

8 lime wedges

1 In large heavy-bottomed saucepan bring water to boil. Add rice and salt; reduce heat to low. Cover and simmer 20 minutes. Remove from heat and let stand, covered, 10 minutes.

2 Add fat-free milk, coconut milk, and brown sugar to rice; stir until blended. Return to low heat and cook, stirring frequently, until mixture is creamy, about 20 minutes. Stir in orange flower water and spoon into 8 (6-ounce) custard cups or ramekins. Cool to room temperature, cover, and refrigerate until chilled, at least 4 hours.

3 To serve, run thin knife around side of ramekin and invert puddings onto 8 serving plates. Sprinkle evenly with coconut and serve with lime wedges.

Per serving (1 pudding and 1½ teaspoons coconut): 146 Cal, 5 g Total Fat, 1 g Sat Fat, 0 g Trans Fat, 1 mg Chol, 171 mg Sod, 24 g Carb, 12 g Sugar, 1 g Fib, 3 g Prot, 70 mg Calc.

STORE AND SERVE LATER

The puddings may be prepared through step 2 and refrigerated up to 3 days. Continue with step 3 just before serving.

Brûléed Cherry-Vanilla Tapioca Pudding Serves 6

- ▲ 2³/4 cups fat-free milk
- ▲ 1 large egg, beaten
- ¹/3 cup plus 6 teaspoons sugar
- 3 tablespoons minute tapioca
- ¹/2 vanilla bean, split in half lengthwise
- ³/4 cup dried sour cherries

1 Combine milk, egg, ¹/3 cup sugar, tapioca, and vanilla bean in medium saucepan; let stand 5 minutes. Bring to boil over medium heat, stirring constantly. Stir in cherries and remove from heat. Let cool 20 minutes. Remove and discard vanilla bean.

2 Spoon pudding evenly into 6 (8-ounce) ramekins. Cool to room temperature, cover, and refrigerate until chilled, at least 2 hours.

3 Preheat broiler. Sprinkle each pudding with 1 teaspoon of remaining sugar. Place ramekins on baking sheet. Broil 2 inches from heat until sugar melts and browns, about 2 minutes. Serve at once.

Per serving (1 ramekin): 160 Cal, 1 g Total Fat, 0 g Sat Fat, 0 g Trans Fat, 38 mg Chol, 58 mg Sod, 34 g Carb, 23 g Sugar, 4 g Fib, 5 g Prot, 151 mg Calc.

STORE AND SERVE LATER
The puddings may be prepared through step 2 and refrigerated up to 1 day. Continue with step 3 just before serving.

Blackberry-Ginger Yogurt Swirl Pops Serves 6

- ▲ 1 **cup blackberries**
- 1 **tablespoon confectioners' sugar**
- 1 **(14-ounce) container low-fat frozen vanilla yogurt, softened**
- 2 **tablespoons finely chopped crystallized ginger**

1 Puree blackberries and sugar in food processor. Pour mixture through strainer into small bowl and press down with rubber spatula to extract as much liquid as possible. Discard solids.

2 Place yogurt in large bowl. Add blackberry puree and ginger. Gently stir to create marbled effect. Spoon into 6 small paper cups; cover with foil. Insert popsicle stick into center of each cup through foil. Freeze until completely frozen, at least 6 hours. To serve, remove foil and lift ice pops from cups.

Per serving (1 ice pop): 156 Cal, 3 g Total Fat, 2 g Sat Fat, 0 g Trans Fat, 41 mg Chol, 36 mg Sod, 27 g Carb, 17 g Sugar, 1 g Fib, 6 g Prot, 169 mg Calc.

STORE AND SERVE LATER
The ice pops may be frozen up to 2 months.

Blackberry-Ginger Yogurt Swirl Pops and Honeydew-Lime Pops, 154

Honeydew-Lime Pops Serves 8

▲ 4   **cups cubed ripe honeydew**

½   **cup superfine sugar**

1   **teaspoon grated lime zest**

⅓   **cup fresh lime juice**

¼   **cup water**

1 Puree all ingredients in food processor.

2 Spoon into 8 (3-ounce) ice pop molds. Cover molds with tops. Freeze until completely frozen, at least 6 hours.

Per serving (1 ice pop): 63 Cal, 0 g Total Fat, 0 g Sat Fat, 0 g Trans Fat, 0 mg Chol, 16 mg Sod, 18 g Carb, 16 g Sugar, 1 g Fib, 1 g Prot, 7 mg Calc.

STORE AND SERVE LATER
The ice pops may be frozen up to 2 months.

Chocolate Cherry Sorbet Serves 8

1 cup water

2 Lapsang Souchong tea bags

1/2 cup dried sour cherries

1 pint chocolate sorbet, softened

▲ 2 cups fresh cherries, pitted

1 Bring water to boil in small saucepan. Add tea bags and cherries. Remove from heat, cover, and let stand 1 hour. Drain, discarding tea bags and liquid. Pulse cherries in food processor until finely chopped.

2 Place sorbet in large bowl. Add cherries and stir until well combined. Transfer to airtight container and freeze until completely frozen, at least 4 hours. Serve sorbet with fresh cherries.

Per serving (1/4 cup sorbet and 1/4 cup cherries): 98 Cal, 0 g Total Fat, 0 g Sat Fat, 0 g Trans Fat, 0 mg Chol, 55 mg Sod, 22 g Carb, 17 g Sugar, 2 g Fib, 1 g Prot, 6 mg Calc.

STORE AND SERVE LATER
The sorbet may be frozen up to 2 months. Serve with 2 cups pitted fresh cherries.

**Vanilla-Berry Terrine with
Chocolate Sauce**

Vanilla-Berry Terrine
with Chocolate Sauce Serves 16

TERRINE

- **8**   **chocolate cookie wafers, crumbled**
- **1**   **pint raspberry sorbet, softened**
- **1**   **pint low-fat vanilla ice cream, softened**
- **1**   **pint strawberry sorbet, softened**

CHOCOLATE SAUCE

- ▲ **1**   **cup fat-free milk**
- **1/4**   **cup water**
- **1/2**   **cup unsweetened cocoa**
- **1/2**   **cup packed dark brown sugar**
- **2**   **teaspoons cornstarch**
- **1**   **teaspoon instant espresso powder**
-   **Pinch salt**
- **1**   **teaspoon vanilla extract**

1   To make terrine, line 9 x 5-inch loaf pan with 2 sheets of plastic wrap, allowing excess to extend over rim by 2 inches.

2   Pulse chocolate wafers in food processor until finely ground. Set aside.

3   With rubber spatula, spread raspberry sorbet evenly in prepared pan, packing it into corners. Sprinkle with half of chocolate crumbs. Top with an even layer of vanilla ice cream. Top ice cream with remaining chocolate crumbs. Top with an even layer of strawberry sorbet. Tightly cover with plastic wrap and then with heavy-duty foil. Freeze until completely frozen, at least 6 hours.

4   Meanwhile, to make sauce, whisk together milk, water, cocoa, brown sugar, cornstarch, espresso powder, and salt in small saucepan and set over medium heat. Cook, stirring often, until mixture comes to boil and thickens, about 8 minutes. Remove from heat and stir in vanilla. Transfer to bowl and let cool. Cover and refrigerate until chilled, at least 1 hour.

5   Remove terrine from freezer and let stand at room temperature about 5 minutes. Invert terrine onto cutting board. Lift off pan and remove plastic wrap. With thin sharp knife, cut terrine crosswise into 1/2-inch-thick slices and place on chilled plates. Drizzle with sauce and serve at once.

Per serving (1/16 of terrine and 1 1/2 tablespoons sauce): 140 Cal, 1 g Total Fat, 1 g Sat Fat, 0 g Trans Fat, 2 mg Chol, 47 mg Sod, 32 g Carb, 25 g Sugar, 2 g Fib, 2 g Prot, 54 mg Calc.

4 PointsPlus® value

STORE AND SERVE LATER
The terrine may be frozen up to 2 months and the sauce may be refrigerated up to 2 days. Continue with step 5 just before serving.

Ricotta Gelato Serves 16

1½ cups superfine sugar

¾ cup water

½ vanilla bean

1 (15-ounce) container part-skim ricotta

▲½ cup fat-free half-and-half

1 teaspoon grated lemon zest

1 teaspoon grated orange zest

1 Combine sugar and water in medium bowl; stir until sugar dissolves.

2 With small, sharp knife, split vanilla bean lengthwise in half and scrape out seeds. Puree vanilla-bean seeds, ricotta, and half-and-half in food processor. Add sugar mixture, lemon zest, and orange zest and pulse until well combined.

3 Pour mixture into ice-cream maker and freeze according to manufacturer's instructions. Transfer to airtight container and freeze until completely frozen, at least 4 hours.

Per serving (¼ cup): 82 Cal, 2 g Total Fat, 1 g Sat Fat, 0 g Trans Fat, 8 mg Chol, 34 mg Sod, 15 g Carb, 14 g Sugar, 0 g Fib, 3 g Prot, 73 mg Calc.

STORE AND SERVE LATER
The gelato may be frozen up to 2 months.

Goat Cheese Cream with Berries and Sauce

Serves 8

1   cup soft goat cheese

³/₄   cup low-fat (2%) cottage cheese

▲ ¹/₂   cup fat-free sour cream

¹/₂   cup confectioners' sugar

1   teaspoon vanilla extract

     Pinch salt

▲ 4   cups fresh raspberries, blackberries, or sliced strawberries

1   Puree goat cheese, cottage cheese, sour cream, confectioners' sugar, vanilla, and salt in food processor. Transfer to an airtight container and refrigerate until chilled, at least 2 hours.

2   To make sauce, wash food processor. Add 1 cup of berries and pulse until smooth. Pour mixture through strainer into small bowl and press down with rubber spatula to extract as much liquid as possible. Discard solids. Transfer to an airtight container and refrigerate until chilled, at least 2 hours.

3   To serve, spoon ¹/₄ cup of goat cheese mixture into 8 bowls, drizzle each with 1 tablespoon raspberry sauce, and top with ¹/₃ cup of remaining raspberries.

Per serving (¹/₃ cup berries, ¹/₄ cup cream, and 1 tablespoon sauce): 169 Cal, 7 g Total Fat, 4 g Sat Fat, 0 g Trans Fat, 17 mg Chol, 216 mg Sod, 18 g Carb, 11 g Sugar, 4 g Fib, 9 g Prot, 94 mg Calc.

STORE AND SERVE LATER

The goat cheese cream and the raspberry sauce may be refrigerated in separate containers up to 2 days. Continue with step 3 to serve.

Frozen Chocolate-Mango Cake Serves 16

½ cup all-purpose flour

½ cup sugar

¼ cup unsweetened cocoa

½ teaspoon baking soda

¼ teaspoon baking powder

¼ teaspoon salt

1 large egg yolk

¼ cup low-fat buttermilk

¼ cup water

1 tablespoon canola oil

1 teaspoon vanilla extract

1 pint mango sorbet, softened

▲ 4 large mangoes, peeled, pitted, and sliced

8 tablespoons chocolate syrup

1 Preheat oven to 350°F. Spray 9-inch springform pan with cooking spray.

2 Whisk together flour, sugar, cocoa, baking soda, baking powder, and salt in large bowl. Whisk together egg yolk, buttermilk, water, oil, and vanilla in medium bowl. Add egg yolk mixture to flour mixture and stir until well blended. Spoon into prepared pan and bake until toothpick inserted in center comes out clean, about 15 minutes. Let cool on wire rack in pan.

3 Spread sorbet over cake in even layer, spreading it all the way to edge. Wrap tightly in heavy-duty foil; freeze until completely frozen, at least 4 hours.

4 To serve, top cake with mango slices and drizzle with chocolate syrup. Cut cake into slices with serrated knife.

Per serving (¹/₁₆ of cake): 137 Cal, 2 g Total Fat, 0 g Sat Fat, 0 g Trans Fat, 13 mg Chol, 100 mg Sod, 33 g Carb, 26 g Sugar, 2 g Fib, 1 g Prot, 16 mg Calc.

STORE AND SERVE LATER
The cake may be prepared through step 3 and frozen for up to 2 months. Continue with step 4 to serve.

Frozen Chocolate-Mango Cake

Orange and Date Compote with Dark Chocolate Serves 4 🕐

▲ 4   navel oranges

½   cup dates, pitted and halved lengthwise

4   teaspoons vanilla sugar or granulated sugar

¼   teaspoon orange flower water or vanilla extract

2   teaspoons grated bittersweet chocolate

1 With sharp knife, peel oranges, removing all white pith. Working over medium bowl, cut between membranes to release segments. Squeeze juice from membranes, then discard membranes. Add dates, sugar, and orange flower water; stir to combine.

2 Serve at room temperature or transfer to an airtight container and refrigerate until chilled, at least 2 hours. Sprinkle with chocolate just before serving.

Per serving (½ cup compote and ½ teaspoon chocolate):
175 Cal, 3 g Total Fat, 2 g Sat Fat, 0 g Trans Fat, 0 mg Chol, 1 mg Sod, 40 g Carb, 31 g Sugar, 5 g Fib, 2 g Prot, 70 mg Calc.

5 PointsPlus® value

STORE AND SERVE LATER
The compote may be refrigerated up to 2 days. Sprinkle with 2 teaspoons grated bittersweet chocolate just before serving.

Honeyed Apricot Compote with Crystallized Ginger Serves 4

2 **cups dried apricots**

1 **cup apricot nectar**

1 **tablespoon honey**

5 **whole cardamom pods, crushed or $1/8$ teaspoon ground cardamom**

▲ 2 **cups fresh raspberries**

2 **teaspoons finely chopped crystallized ginger**

1 Combine apricots, nectar, honey, and cardamom pods in medium saucepan and bring to boil over medium heat. Remove from heat, cover, and let stand 2 hours.

2 Serve at room temperature or transfer to an airtight container and refrigerate until chilled, at least 2 hours. Stir in raspberries and sprinkle with ginger just before serving.

Per serving ($1^1/4$ cups compote and $1/2$ teaspoon ginger): 253 Cal, 1 g Total Fat, 0 g Sat Fat, 0 g Trans Fat, 0 mg Chol, 10 mg Sod, 64 g Carb, 51 g Sugar, 9 g Fib, 3 g Prot, 82 mg Calc.

7 PointsPlus value

STORE AND SERVE LATER
The compote may be refrigerated without the raspberries and crystallized ginger up to 2 days. Stir in the raspberries and sprinkle with the ginger just before serving.

Chocolate Chip–Raisin Energy Bars Serves 24

1   **cup old-fashioned oats**

1/2   **cup pumpkin seeds**

1/2   **cup ground flaxseed**

1/2   **cup shredded unsweetened coconut**

1/2   **cup raisins**

1/2   **cup mini–chocolate chips**

1/2   **cup instant nonfat dry milk**

1/4   **cup white whole wheat flour**

▲ 2   **large eggs**

1/3   **cup honey**

1   Preheat oven to 350°F. Spray 9 x 13-inch baking pan with nonstick spray.

2   Combine oats, pumpkin seeds, and flaxseed in food processor; pulse 3–4 times until finely chopped. Transfer to medium bowl; stir in coconut, raisins, chocolate chips, dry milk, flour, eggs, and honey.

3   Transfer to prepared baking pan and press evenly into pan with dampened fingers. Bake until edges are browned, 20 minutes. Let cool completely in pan on wire rack. Cut into 24 bars.

Per serving (1 bar): 110 Cal, 5 g Total Fat, 2 g Sat Fat, 0 g Trans Fat, 18 mg Chol, 16 mg Sod, 15 g Carb, 9 g Sugar, 2 g Fib, 3 g Prot, 25 mg Calc.

STORE AND SERVE LATER

Place the bars in an airtight container with wax paper between layers and refrigerate up to 1 week or freeze up to 3 months. If frozen, thaw at room temperature.

Sweet-and-Salty Peanut Butter-Banana Bars, 166 and Chocolate Chip–Raisin Energy Bars

Sweet-and-Salty
Peanut Butter–Banana Bars Serves 24

2	cups old-fashioned oats
1	cup dry roasted, salted pumpkin seeds
▲ 4	ripe bananas, mashed
1	cup peanut butter
¼	cup honey
▲ 1	large egg
1	cup dried sour cherries
1	cup miniature whole grain pretzel rounds

1 Preheat oven to 350°F. Line 9 x 13-inch baking pan with foil, allowing foil to extend over rim of pan by 2 inches. Spray with nonstick spray.

2 Spread oats and pumpkin seeds on baking sheet. Bake, stirring once, until toasted, about 12 minutes. Transfer to large plate to cool.

3 Meanwhile, combine bananas, peanut butter, and honey in large saucepan. Set over medium-high heat and cook, stirring constantly, until peanut butter is melted and mixture is blended, about 5 minutes. Transfer banana mixture to large bowl and let cool. Stir in egg. Add oats, pumpkin seeds, cherries, and pretzels and stir until well combined.

4 Spoon batter into prepared pan and spread evenly. Bake until edges are lightly browned, about 20 minutes. Let cool in pan on wire rack 10 minutes. Lift from pan using foil as handles; cool completely on wire rack. Cut into 24 bars.

Per serving (1 bar): 187 Cal, 10 g Total Fat, 2 g Sat Fat, 0 g Trans Fat, 8 mg Chol, 58 mg Sod, 21 g Carb, 9 g Sugar, 4 g Fib, 6 g Prot, 10 mg Calc.

STORE AND SERVE LATER
Place the bars in an airtight container with wax paper between layers and refrigerate up to 1 week or freeze up to 3 months. If frozen, thaw at room temperature overnight.

Anise Cookies Makes 36

1½ cups all-purpose flour

1½ cups white whole wheat flour

½ cup sugar

1 tablespoon anise seeds

½ cup extra-virgin olive oil

½ cup dry white wine

▲ 1 large egg

1 Preheat oven to 350°F. Line baking sheets with parchment paper.

2 Combine all-purpose and whole wheat flours, sugar, and anise seeds in work bowl of stand mixer with paddle attachment, or if mixing by hand, combine in large bowl.

3 Whisk together oil, wine, and egg in small bowl until well blended. Add oil mixture to flour mixture and beat on low speed or stir with wooden spoon until stiff dough forms.

4 Scoop dough into rounded tablespoon portions on work surface. Using hands, roll each portion on work surface into a 3-inch rope. Bring ends of each rope together and press firmly to create ring. Place rings 1 inch apart on prepared baking sheets.

5 Bake until lightly browned, about 25 minutes. Let cool on baking sheets on wire racks about 1 minute. Transfer cookies to racks and let cool completely.

Per serving (1 cookie): 78 Cal, 3 g Total Fat, 1 g Sat Fat, 0 g Trans Fat, 6 mg Chol, 2 mg Sod, 10 g Carb, 2 g Sugar, 1 g Fib, 1 g Prot, 2 mg Calc.

STORE AND SERVE LATER
Place the cookies in an airtight container and store at room temperature up to 1 week or freeze up to 3 months. If frozen, thaw at room temperature overnight.

Sesame Meringues Makes 50

▲ 3 large egg whites

¾ cup sugar

10 individually wrapped
    sesame crunch candies,
    crushed

1 Preheat oven to 300°F. Line baking sheets with parchment paper.

2 Place egg whites in medium bowl and beat with electric mixer on medium-high speed until soft peaks form. Slowly beat in sugar; continue beating until meringue is glossy and holds stiff peaks. Gently fold 3 tablespoons crushed candies into egg white mixture with rubber spatula.

3 Drop mixture by rounded teaspoons onto prepared baking sheets. Sprinkle with remaining crushed candies. Bake until meringues are lightly browned, about 25 minutes. Turn oven off; leave meringues in oven until meringues are dried and crisped, about 1 hour. Remove from oven and cool completely on baking sheets on wire racks.

Per serving (2 cookies): 20 Cal, 0 g Total Fat, 0 g Sat Fat, 0 g Trans Fat, 0 mg Chol, 14 mg Sod, 5 g Carb, 5 g Sugar, 0 g Fib, 1 g Prot, 5 mg Calc.

STORE AND SERVE LATER
Place the cookies in an airtight container and store at room temperature up to 1 week.

Almond-Ginger Biscotti Makes 28

1³/₄ cups all-purpose flour

¹/₂ cup slivered almonds

¹/₄ cup minced crystallized ginger

¹/₂ cup yellow cornmeal

1 tablespoon baking powder

¹/₄ teaspoon salt

1 cup sugar

▲ 2 large eggs, lightly beaten

▲ 2 tablespoons fat-free milk

¹/₂ teaspoon vanilla extract

1 Preheat oven to 350°F. Spray two baking sheets with nonstick spray.

2 Whisk together flour, almonds, ginger, cornmeal, baking powder, and salt in large bowl. Whisk together sugar, eggs, milk, and vanilla extract in medium bowl. With electric mixer on low speed, beat sugar mixture into flour mixture until dough forms.

3 Gather dough with your hands and place on lightly floured surface. Shape into log about 14 inches long; transfer log to one of the prepared baking sheets and pat dough gently until it is about 3 inches wide and ³/₄ inch thick. Bake until dough is firm to touch and toothpick inserted into center of log comes out clean, about 20 minutes. Reduce oven temperature to 300°F.

4 Transfer log to cutting board and let cool about 5 minutes. Cut log with serrated knife into ¹/₂-inch-thick slices. Arrange slices in single layer on prepared baking sheets. Bake biscotti 10 minutes; turn over and bake 10 minutes longer. Cool completely on wire rack; biscotti will crisp as they cool.

Per serving (2 cookies): 167 Cal, 3 g Total Fat, 0 g Sat Fat, 0 g Trans Fat, 27 mg Chol, 139 mg Sod, 32 g Carb, 15 g Sugar, 1 g Fib, 4 g Prot, 72 mg Calc.

STORE AND SERVE LATER
Place the biscotti in an airtight container and store at room temperature up to 2 weeks.

Bonus

Double Duty Dinners

Use these recipes to make
a delicious dinner one night, then
store part of it to make a completely
different meal later in the week.
You'll make the most of your time
in the kitchen, yet never feel like
you're having leftovers.

Grilled Flank Steak with Asian Coleslaw
Serves 4 plus leftovers

½ cup reduced-fat Asian sesame dressing

2 garlic cloves, minced

1 tablespoon grated peeled fresh ginger

▲ 1 (2-pound) lean flank steak, trimmed

▲ 8 cups thinly sliced Napa cabbage (about 1½ pounds)

▲ 1 (10-ounce) bag shredded carrots

▲ 1 small red onion, thinly sliced

▲ 6 scallions, thinly sliced

1 Stir together dressing, garlic, and ginger in small bowl. Transfer 3 tablespoons of dressing mixture to zip-close plastic bag; add steak. Squeeze out air and seal bag; turn to coat steak. Refrigerate, turning bag occasionally, at least 2 hours or overnight.

2 Combine cabbage, carrots, onion, and scallions in large bowl; toss to mix well. Transfer half of cabbage mixture (about 6 cups) to large zip-close bag and refrigerate up to 4 days for later use in Beef Lo Mein, opposite. Add remaining dressing mixture to remaining cabbage mixture; toss to coat. Cover and refrigerate coleslaw until ready to serve.

3 Spray grill rack with nonstick spray and prepare medium-hot fire. Place steak on grill rack and grill until an instant-read thermometer inserted into side of steak registers 145°F for medium, 8–9 minutes on each side. Transfer steak to cutting board and cover loosely with foil. Let stand 5 minutes.

4 Cut steak crosswise in half. Wrap and refrigerate half of steak up to 4 days for later use in Beef Lo Mein, opposite. Cut remaining steak across grain into 16 slices. Serve steak with coleslaw.

Per serving (4 slices steak with 1½ cups coleslaw): 229 Cal, 8 g Total Fat, 3 g Sat Fat, 0 g Trans Fat, 42 mg Chol, 403 mg Sod, 12 g Carb, 7 g Sugar, 3 g Fib, 26 g Prot, 83 mg Calc.

FOR YOUR INFO
If you're tight on time, you can use 2 (14-ounce) bags coleslaw mix instead of the Napa cabbage and carrots.

Beef Lo Mein Serves 4 🕐

▲ 4   **ounces 100% buckwheat soba noodles**

3   **tablespoons hoisin sauce**

2   **tablespoons water**

1   **teaspoon reduced-sodium soy sauce**

1   **teaspoon green jalapeño sauce**

1   **pound reserved cooked steak and 6 cups reserved coleslaw mixture from Grilled Flank Steak with Asian Coleslaw (opposite)**

2   **teaspoons canola oil**

2   **garlic cloves, minced**

▲ 1   **(5-ounce) package shiitake mushrooms, stems removed and sliced**

1   Cook soba noodles according to package directions. Drain and rinse noodles in cold water. Whisk together hoisin sauce, water, soy sauce, and jalapeño sauce in a small bowl. Thinly slice steak.

2   Heat oil in large nonstick skillet over medium-high heat. Add garlic and cook, stirring constantly, until fragrant, 30 seconds. Add mushrooms and reserved coleslaw mixture; cook, stirring occasionally, until softened, about 5 minutes.

3   Add hoisin sauce mixture to skillet, and cook, stirring often, until mixture simmers, 1 minute. Add noodles and steak; cook, stirring often, until heated through, about 2 minutes.

Per serving (about 1¼ cups lo mein): 371 Cal, 10 g Total Fat, 3 g Sat Fat, 0 g Trans Fat, 42 mg Chol, 641 mg Sod, 41 g Carb, 9 g Sugar, 4 g Fib, 31 g Prot, 101 mg Calc.

FOR YOUR INFO
To add more vegetables to the lo mein, add a thinly sliced red bell pepper to the cooking water when you cook the soba noodles. The pepper will cook in the same time as the soba noodles.

Pairs Well With: Cucumber Salad with Miso Dressing, page 87

Grilled Sirloin with Black Cherry Sauce
Serves 4 plus leftovers

▲ 1 **(2-pound) boneless lean sirloin, trimmed**

¼ **teaspoon salt**

¼ **teaspoon pepper**

2 **teaspoons olive oil**

2 **shallots, minced**

▲ ½ **cup reduced-sodium chicken broth**

½ **cup all-fruit black cherry preserves**

1 **tablespoon balsamic vinegar**

½ **teaspoon hot sauce**

1 Sprinkle steak with salt and pepper. Spray grill rack with nonstick spray and prepare medium-hot fire. Place steak on grill rack and grill until an instant-read thermometer inserted into side of steak registers 145°F for medium, 7–8 minutes on each side. Transfer steak to cutting board and cover loosely with foil. Let stand 5 minutes.

2 Heat oil in medium skillet over medium-high heat. Add shallots and cook, stirring often, until softened and browned, about 4 minutes. Add broth; bring to boil and cook 1 minute. Add fruit preserves and vinegar; return to boil. Reduce heat and simmer, stirring occasionally, until thickened, about 2 minutes. Transfer ¼ cup of sauce to small bowl; cover and refrigerate up to 4 days for later use in Steak and Spinach Salad with Blue Cheese. Stir hot sauce into remaining sauce.

3 Cut steak crosswise in half. Wrap and refrigerate half of steak up to 4 days for later use in Steak and Spinach Salad with Blue Cheese, opposite. Cut remaining steak across grain into 12 slices. Serve with remaining sauce.

Per serving (3 slices steak and 2 tablespoons sauce): 253 Cal, 7 g Total Fat, 2 g Sat Fat, 0 g Trans Fat, 49 mg Chol, 151 mg Sod, 21 g Carb, 17 g Sugar, 0 g Fib, 27 g Prot, 24 mg Calc.

FOR YOUR INFO

To make a quick grilled vegetable to serve with the steak, cut zucchini into lengthwise slices and lightly spray with nonstick spray. Place on the grill rack and grill, until crisp-tender, 1 minute on each side.

Pairs Well With: Maple-Orange Sweet Potatoes, page 37

Steak and Spinach Salad with Blue Cheese Serves 4 🕐

1	**pound cooked steak and ¹⁄₄ cup sauce from** Grilled Sirloin with Black Cherry Sauce **(opposite)**
1	**tablespoon lemon juice**
1	**tablespoon water**
2	**teaspoons Dijon mustard**
¹⁄₄	**teaspoon pepper**
▲ 1	**(9-ounce) package baby spinach**
▲ 2	**cups sliced crimini mushrooms**
▲ 1	**cup halved cherry tomatoes**
▲ 1	**small thinly sliced red onion**
¹⁄₄	**cup crumbled blue cheese**

1 Thinly slice steak. To make dressing, whisk together reserved sauce, lemon juice, water, mustard, and pepper in small bowl.

2 Combine spinach, mushrooms, tomatoes, onion, and sliced steak in large serving bowl; toss to combine. Sprinkle with blue cheese. Serve with dressing.

Per serving (2 cups salad and 1 ¹⁄₂ tablespoons dressing):
296 Cal, 9 g Total Fat, 4 g Sat Fat, 0 g Trans Fat, 59 mg Chol, 427 mg Sod, 22 g Carb, 11 g Sugar, 4 g Fib, 34 g Prot, 181 mg Calc.

7 PointsPlus value

FOR YOUR INFO
To make a small amount of the blue cheese go a long way, crumble the cheese when it is very cold. You'll be able to break it into smaller pieces, so you can spread the delicious flavor throughout the whole salad.

Garlic-Ginger Beef and Vegetable Stir-Fry

Serves 4 plus leftovers

- ▲ 2 **cups instant brown rice**
- ▲ ¼ **cup reduced-sodium chicken broth**
- 3 **tablespoons reduced-sodium teriyaki sauce**
- 1 **tablespoon cornstarch**
- 3 **garlic cloves, minced**
- 1 **tablespoon grated peeled fresh ginger**
- ▲ 1 **(1½ pound) lean flank steak, trimmed and thinly sliced**
- 2 **teaspoons canola oil**
- ▲ 1¼ **pounds baby bok choy, trimmed, quartered, and sliced**
- ▲ 2 **carrots, sliced**
- ▲ 2 **yellow bell peppers, sliced**
- ▲ 1 **(10-ounce) package mushrooms, sliced**
- ▲ 1 **bunch scallions, sliced**

1 Cook rice according to package directions. Transfer half of cooked rice (about 2 cups) to container and let cool. Cover and refrigerate up to 4 days for later use in Steak Fried Rice, opposite.

2 Meanwhile, whisk together broth, teriyaki sauce, cornstarch, garlic, and ginger in small bowl. Set aside.

3 Heat nonstick wok or large deep nonstick skillet over medium-high heat until drop of water sizzles on it. Spray wok with nonstick cooking spray. Add beef in three batches, stir-fry until browned, 3–4 minutes, spraying wok with nonstick spray between batches. Transfer beef to large bowl.

4 Add 1 teaspoon of oil to wok. Add bok choy and carrots. Stir-fry until vegetables are crisp-tender, 6 minutes; transfer to bowl with beef.

5 Add remaining 1 teaspoon oil to wok. Add bell peppers, mushrooms, and scallions. Stir-fry until vegetables are crisp-tender, 4 minutes. Return beef mixture to wok. Stir teriyaki mixture and add to wok. Cook, stirring constantly, until mixture bubbles and thickens, about 1 minute.

6 Transfer 3 cups of stir-fry mixture to container, let cool, and cover. Refrigerate up to 4 days for later use in Steak Fried Rice, opposite. Divide remaining stir-fry mixture and remaining half of rice evenly among 4 plates.

Per serving (1¼ cups stir-fry and ½ cup brown rice): 312 Cal, 9 g Total Fat, 3 g Sat Fat, 0 g Trans Fat, 39 mg Chol, 427 mg Sod, 30 g Carb, 6 g Sugar, 4 g Fib, 28 g Prot, 128 mg Calc.

FOR YOUR INFO
Baby bok choy has a delicate flavor and tender texture, but if you can't find it, you can use 3 cups thinly sliced Napa cabbage or green cabbage in this recipe instead.

Steak Fried Rice Serves 4 🕐

3 cups reserved cooked beef and vegetable mixture and 2 cups reserved cooked brown rice from Garlic-Ginger Beef and Vegetable Stir-Fry (opposite)

▲ 1 large egg

▲ 1 large egg white

1 teaspoon canola oil

1 tablespoon reduced-sodium soy sauce

1 Chop reserved cooked beef and vegetable mixture into ¹/₂-inch pieces. Whisk together egg and egg white in small bowl.

2 Spray large nonstick skillet with nonstick spray and set over medium heat. Add egg mixture, and cook, stirring constantly, until scrambled, about 1 minute. Transfer to plate. Wipe out skillet.

3 Add oil to skillet and set over medium heat. Add beef and vegetable mixture; cook, stirring often, until heated through, about 2 minutes. Add rice, egg mixture, and soy sauce; cook, stirring constantly, until heated through, about 2 minutes.

Per serving (1¹/₄ cups): 250 Cal, 7 g Total Fat, 2 g Sat Fat, 0 g Trans Fat, 74 mg Chol, 419 mg Sod, 27 g Carb, 4 g Sugar, 3 g Fib, 19 g Prot, 79 mg Calc.

FOR YOUR INFO
If you'd like more vegetables in the fried rice, add 2 cups baby spinach when you add the beef and vegetable mixture.

Finish With: Nectarines with Raspberry-Yogurt Sauce, page 130

Grain & Pasta Sides to Serve 4

Brown Rice, Squash, and Scallion Stir-Fry

Heat **2 teaspoons Asian (dark) sesame oil** in large nonstick skillet over medium-high heat. Add **1 yellow squash, diced** and **2 scallions, thinly sliced.** Cook, stirring constantly, until crisp-tender, about 2 minutes. Add **1 (8.8-ounce) package cooked brown rice** (about 1³⁄₄ cups); cook, stirring constantly, until heated through, about 2 minutes. Transfer to serving bowl and stir in **2 tablespoons chopped fresh cilantro** and **2 teaspoons reduced-sodium soy sauce.**

Basil-Barley with Cherry Tomatoes and Feta

Heat **2 teaspoons olive oil** in saucepan over medium-high heat. Add **1 small onion, diced** and **1 garlic clove, minced.** Cook, until softened, 3 minutes. Add **1³⁄₄ cups chicken broth, ¹⁄₂ cup pearl barley, ¹⁄₄ teaspoon salt,** and **¹⁄₄ teaspoon black pepper.** Bring to boil. Cover, reduce heat, and simmer until barley is tender, 25 minutes. Remove from heat and stir in **1 cup cherry tomatoes, halved** and **2 tablespoons minced fresh basil.** Spoon barley into serving dish; sprinkle with **2 tablespoons crumbled feta cheese.**

Orzo with Corn and Bell Pepper

Cook **¹⁄₂ cup whole wheat orzo** according to package directions. Meanwhile, heat **2 teaspoons olive oil** in large nonstick skillet over medium-high heat. Add **1 small red bell pepper, diced** and cook, stirring often, until pepper is softened, about 3 minutes. Add **¹⁄₂ cup frozen corn kernels, 2 tablespoons water,** and **¹⁄₂ teaspoon ground cumin.** Cover and cook until corn is heated through, about 3 minutes. Add orzo, **1 scallion, thinly sliced, ¹⁄₂ teaspoon salt,** and **¹⁄₄ teaspoon black pepper** and cook, stirring often, until heated through, about 2 minutes. Stir in **2 tablespoons chopped fresh cilantro.**

Polenta with Goat Cheese and Chives

PER SERVING

Bring **2 cups reduced-sodium chicken broth** to boil in medium saucepan. Slowly pour in **½ cup instant polenta** in thin steady stream, whisking constantly. Cook, whisking constantly, until thick and creamy, about 5 minutes. Remove from heat and stir in **2 ounces crumbled goat cheese, 1 tablespoon minced fresh chives, ¼ teaspoon salt, and ⅛ teaspoon black pepper.**

Quinoa Pilaf with Tomatoes and Spinach

PER SERVING

Heat **2 teaspoons olive oil** large nonstick skillet over medium-high heat. Add **1 small onion, diced, and 1 garlic clove, minced.** Cook, stirring often, until softened, about 3 minutes. Add **1 cup reduced-sodium chicken broth, ½ cup rinsed quinoa,** and **¼ teaspoon salt.** Bring to boil. Cover, reduce heat, and simmer until quinoa is tender, about 15 minutes. Add **1 cup baby spinach** and **1 plum tomato, chopped;** stir until spinach is wilted, about 1 minute.

Brown Rice with Pear and Pecans

PER SERVING

Heat **2 teaspoons olive oil** in large nonstick skillet over medium heat. Add **1 small onion, diced.** Cover and cook, stirring often, until onion is tender, about 8 minutes. Add **1 garlic clove, minced,** and cook, stirring constantly, until fragrant, 30 seconds. Add **1 (8.8-ounce) package cooked brown rice** (about 1¾ cups), **1 Bartlett pear, cored and diced, 1 teaspoon minced fresh rosemary, ¼ teaspoon salt, and ⅛ teaspoon black pepper.** Cook, stirring often, until heated through, about 2 minutes. Spoon rice into serving dish; sprinkle with **2 tablespoons chopped toasted pecans.**

Couscous-Carrot Pilaf

PER SERVING

Heat **2 teaspoons olive oil** in medium skillet over medium heat. Add **1 carrot, diced,** and **1 shallot, minced,** and cook, stirring often, until softened, about 5 minutes. Add **1¼ cups reduced-sodium chicken broth, 1 cup whole wheat couscous, ¼ teaspoon ground cumin, ¼ teaspoon ground coriander,** and **⅛ teaspoon black pepper.** Bring to boil. Cover, remove from heat, and let stand 5 minutes. Stir in **2 tablespoons minced fresh flat-leaf parsley.**

Herbed Parmesan-Garlic Pasta

PER SERVING

Cook **6 ounces whole wheat linguine or fettuccine** according to package directions. Heat **2 teaspoons olive oil** in large nonstick skillet over medium heat. Add **2 cloves minced garlic** and cook, stirring constantly, just until garlic begins to brown. Add pasta and toss to coat. Remove from heat and stir in **3 tablespoons minced fresh flat-leaf parsley, basil, or dill,** or a combination, **¼ cup grated Parmesan, ¼ teaspoon salt,** and **⅛ teaspoon black pepper** and toss to coat.

Chili-Orange Glazed Pork Tenderloin and Peppers Serves 4 plus leftovers

▲ 3 **large red bell peppers, cut into 1¹⁄₂-inch strips**

▲ 2 **(1-pound) lean pork tenderloins, trimmed**

2 **tablespoons all-fruit orange marmalade**

2 **tablespoons apple cider vinegar**

1 **seeded and finely chopped chipotle en adobo**

1 **teaspoon grated orange zest**

1 Preheat oven to 475°F. Spray heavy rimmed baking pan with nonstick spray.

2 Place bell peppers in prepared pan.

3 Spray 9 x 13-inch baking dish with nonstick spray; place pork tenderloins in baking dish. Whisk together marmalade, vinegar, chipotle en adobo, and orange zest in small bowl. Transfer 2 tablespoons of marmalade mixture to small container; cover and refrigerate for later use in Pork and Black Beans with Rice, opposite. Brush remaining glaze evenly over pork.

4 Roast peppers until well browned and tender, stirring once, 20–25 minutes. Roast pork until instant-read thermometer inserted into centers of tenderloins registers 145°F, about 20 minutes. Transfer pork to cutting board and cover loosely with foil. Let stand 10 minutes.

5 Transfer 1 tenderloin and one-third of peppers (about ¹⁄₂ cup) to container and let cool. Cover and refrigerate up to 4 days for later use in Pork and Black Beans with Rice, opposite. Cut pork into 12 slices and serve with remaining peppers.

Per serving (3 slices pork and scant ¹⁄₄ cup pepper slices):
163 Cal, 3 g Total Fat, 1 g Sat Fat, 0 g Trans Fat, 62 mg Chol, 63 mg Sod, 8 g Carb, 6 g Sugar, 2 g Fib, 23 g Prot, 11 mg Calc.

FOR YOUR INFO
While you roast the peppers and pork, make baked potatoes to serve alongside. To do so, prick 4 small baking potatoes several times with a fork and place in a medium baking pan. Place in the oven about 20 minutes before you put the peppers in the oven. Bake the potatoes until tender, 50 minutes to 1 hour. The per-serving *PointsPlus* value will increase by *3*.

Pork and Black Beans with Rice Serves 4 ⏲

2 teaspoons canola oil

▲ 1 small onion, chopped

▲ 1 jalapeño, seeded and finely chopped

1 tablespoon ground cumin

▲ 1 (15-ounce) can reduced-sodium black beans, rinsed and drained

1/2 cup reserved red bell pepper slices, chopped, 1 reserved pork tenderloin, cut into 1/2-inch cubes, and 2 tablespoons glaze from Chili-Orange Glazed Pork Tenderloin and Peppers (opposite)

1/4 cup water

▲ 2 cups hot cooked brown rice

1 Heat oil in large nonstick skillet over medium-high heat. Add onion and jalapeño; cook, stirring frequently, until softened, 4 minutes. Add cumin and cook, stirring constantly, until fragrant, 30 seconds. Stir in black beans, bell pepper, and pork.

2 Add glaze and water to skillet; stir until well combined. Reduce heat to low and cook, stirring frequently, until heated through, about 5 minutes. Serve with rice.

Per serving (about 1 cup pork mixture and 1/2 cup rice):
352 Cal, 7 g Total Fat, 1 g Sat Fat, 0 g Trans Fat, 62 mg Chol, 285 mg Sod, 46 g Carb, 6 g Sugar, 9 g Fib, 30 g Prot, 69 mg Calc.

9 PointsPlus® value

FOR YOUR INFO
To make this dish even more flavorful, sprinkle each serving with chopped fresh cilantro and thinly sliced scallions.

Pairs Well With: **Lemony Spinach and Avocado Salad, page 86**

Apple Marinated Pork Chops with Cabbage

Serves 4 plus leftovers

3   **cups unsweetened apple juice**

2   **teaspoons pickling spices**

▲ 7   **(5-ounce) lean bone-in pork loin chops, trimmed**

1   **tablespoon canola oil**

▲ 1   **large sweet onion, thinly sliced**

▲ 1   **(2-pound) Savoy cabbage, trimmed and cut into 1¹/₂-inch wedges**

▲ 1   **(14¹/₂-ounce) can reduced-sodium chicken broth**

1   **tablespoon minced fresh thyme or 1 teaspoon dried**

¹/₄   **teaspoon kosher salt**

▲ 2   **large Braeburn or Rome apples, cored and thickly sliced**

2   **teaspoons Dijon mustard**

1   **teaspoon honey**

1   Bring apple juice and pickling spices to boil in saucepan; remove from heat. Add 1 cup ice cubes and let cool 10 minutes. Place pork chops in large shallow dish. Add apple juice mixture, adding cold water, if necessary to cover chops. Cover and refrigerate at least 4 hours or up to overnight.

2   Preheat oven to 350°F. Spray large rimmed baking pan with nonstick spray.

3   Remove pork chops from marinade; discard marinade. Pat dry with paper towels. Spray large nonstick skillet with nonstick spray and set over medium-high heat. Add pork chops in batches; cook, turning once, until lightly browned, 2 minutes.

4   Transfer pork to prepared baking pan. Bake until instant-read thermometer inserted into side of each chop registers 145°F, 8–10 minutes. Transfer 3 pork chops to container and let cool. Cover and refrigerate up to 4 days for later use in African Pork and Vegetable Stew, opposite.

5   Meanwhile, heat oil in large deep nonstick skillet over medium-high heat; add onion and cook until softened, 5 minutes. Add cabbage, broth, thyme, and salt; bring to boil. Reduce heat and simmer, covered, 10 minutes.

6   Add apples to skillet; cover and simmer until apples are tender, about 8 minutes. Transfer 4 cups of cabbage mixture to container and let cool. Cover and refrigerate up to 4 days for later use in African Pork and Vegetable Stew, opposite.

7   Stir together mustard and honey in small bowl. Place pork chops on 4 plates; divide remaining cabbage mixture among plates. Drizzle cabbage evenly with mustard mixture.

Per serving (1 pork chop, 1¹/₄ cups cabbage mixture, and ³/₄ teaspoon mustard mixture): 254 Cal, 8 g Total Fat, 2 g Sat Fat, 0 g Trans Fat, 59 mg Chol, 222 mg Sod, 25 g Carb, 15 g Sugar, 6 g Fib, 23 g Prot, 77 mg Calc.

African Pork and Vegetable Stew Serves 4 🕐

- **2** teaspoons canola oil
- **2** shallots, minced
- **2** teaspoons ground cumin
- **1** teaspoon turmeric
- **¼** teaspoon cinnamon
- ▲ **2** cups peeled and cubed butternut squash
- ▲ **1** cup reduced-sodium chicken broth
- **¼** teaspoon salt
- **3** reserved pork chops, cut into thin strips, and 4 cups reserved cabbage mixture from **Apple Marinated Pork Chops with Cabbage (opposite)**

1 Heat oil in large nonstick skillet over medium-high heat. Add shallots and cook, stirring constantly, until browned, 3 minutes. Add cumin, turmeric, and cinnamon; cook, stirring constantly, until fragrant, 30 seconds.

2 Add squash, broth, and salt; bring to boil. Reduce heat and simmer, covered, until squash is just tender, about 8 minutes. Stir in pork and cabbage mixture. Cover and cook, stirring occasionally, until heated through, about 5 minutes.

Per serving (1¾ cups): 264 Cal, 9 g Total Fat, 2 g Sat Fat, 0 g Trans Fat, 44 mg Chol, 300 mg Sod, 30 g Carb, 13 g Sugar, 7 g Fib, 20 g Prot, 104 mg Calc.

FOR YOUR INFO

If you have leftover butternut squash from preparing this recipe, steam the cubed squash until tender and serve it as a side dish later in the week.

Finish With: Molasses-Spice Roasted Pears, page 131

Lamb Chops and Barley with Mint Sauce Serves 4 plus leftovers

- ▲ 1/3 cup quick-cooking barley
- 2 cups fresh mint leaves
- 1 cup fresh flat-leaf parsley
- 1/4 cup water
- 3 garlic cloves
- ▲ 1 small jalapeño, seeded
- 1 tablespoon olive oil
- 1 teaspoon lime zest
- 1 tablespoon lime juice
- 1/4 teaspoon salt
- 1/4 teaspoon ground cumin
- 1/4 teaspoon pepper
- ▲ 14 (2 3/4-ounce) bone-in lean loin lamb chops, trimmed

1 Prepare barley according to package directions.

2 Meanwhile, to make sauce, puree mint, parsley, water, garlic, jalapeño, oil, lime zest, lime juice, salt, cumin and black pepper in food processor. Transfer 1/4 cup of mint sauce to container; cover and refrigerate up to 4 days for later use in Lamb, Chickpea, and Cauliflower Curry, opposite.

3 Spray grill rack with nonstick spray and prepare medium-hot fire. Place lamb chops on grill rack and grill until an instant-read thermometer inserted into side of lamb registers 145°F for medium, 5–6 minutes on each side. Transfer 8 lamb chops to platter and cover loosely with foil. Let stand 5 minutes. Transfer 6 lamb chops to container and let cool. Cover and refrigerate up to 4 days for later use in Lamb, Chickpea, and Cauliflower Curry, opposite.

4 Stir 1 tablespoon of mint sauce into prepared barley. Serve lamb chops with barley and remaining mint sauce.

Per serving (2 lamb chops, 1/2 cup barley, and 1 tablespoon mint sauce): 236 Cal, 7 g Total Fat, 2 g Sat Fat, 0 g Trans Fat, 62 mg Chol, 135 mg Sod, 19 g Carb, 0 g Sugar, 4 g Fib, 23 g Prot, 50 mg Calc.

6 PointsPlus value

FOR YOUR INFO
While you grill the lamb chops, grill some tomatoes to serve alongside. To do so, cut the tomatoes into wedges and lightly spray with cooking spray. Grill the tomatoes until lightly browned and heated through, about 5 minutes. Sprinkle with grated lime zest, salt, and pepper.

Lamb, Chickpea, and Cauliflower Curry Serves 4 ⏱

2   teaspoons canola oil

▲ 1   onion, diced

3   garlic cloves, minced

1   tablespoon curry powder

2   teaspoons grated peeled fresh ginger

½   teaspoon sugar

¼   cup water

2   teaspoons cornstarch

▲ 1   (14½-ounce) can chicken broth

▲ 3   cups cauliflower florets

▲ 2   carrots, sliced

▲ 1   (15½-ounce) can chickpeas, rinsed

6   reserved cooked lamb chops, boned and chopped, and ¼ cup reserved mint sauce from Lamb Chops and Barley with Mint Sauce (opposite)

1   Heat oil in large nonstick skillet over medium-high heat. Add onion and cook, stirring often, until browned, about 4 minutes. Add garlic, curry powder, ginger, and sugar; cook, stirring constantly, until fragrant, 30 seconds.

2   Stir together water and cornstarch in small bowl. Add cornstarch mixture and broth to skillet; bring to boil. Cook, stirring constantly, 1 minute. Add cauliflower and carrots. Reduce heat to medium; cover and cook until vegetables are crisp-tender, about 6 minutes.

3   Add chickpeas and lamb; cover and cook until heated through, 4–5 minutes. Ladle stew into 4 bowls; drizzle evenly with mint sauce.

Per serving (1½ cups curry and 1 tablespoon mint sauce): 314 Cal, 11 g Total Fat, 2 g Sat Fat, 0 g Trans Fat, 47 mg Chol, 443 mg Sod, 32 g Carb, 8 g Sugar, 8 g Fib, 24 g Prot, 109 mg Calc.

8 PointsPlus value

FOR YOUR INFO

Chickpeas are commonly used for making curry dishes, but if you have cannellini beans or small white beans on hand, you can use those instead.

Grilled Chicken with White Bean Ratatouille

Serves 4 plus leftovers

1	tablespoon olive oil
3	garlic cloves, minced
¼	teaspoon salt
▲ 7	(5-ounce) skinless boneless chicken breasts
▲ 2	small eggplants, quartered lengthwise
▲ 2	zucchini, halved lengthwise
▲ 2	yellow squash, halved lengthwise
▲ 1	sweet onion, cut into ½-inch-thick slices
▲ 3	plum tomatoes, chopped
▲ 1	(15½-ounce) can cannellini (white kidney) beans, rinsed and drained
¼	cup chopped fresh basil
3	tablespoons red-wine vinegar

1 Combine oil, garlic, and salt in large zip-close plastic bag; add chicken. Squeeze out air and seal bag; turn to coat chicken. Refrigerate, turning occasionally, 1 hour or up to 4 hours.

2 Spray grill rack with nonstick spray; preheat grill to medium or prepare medium fire.

3 Combine eggplant, zucchini, yellow squash, and onion in large bowl; lightly spray with nonstick spray. Place vegetables on grill rack and grill, turning often, until softened and browned, about 15 minutes. Transfer half of vegetables (about 3 ½ cups) to container and let cool. Cover and refrigerate up to 2 days for later use in Chicken Pan Bagnat, opposite.

4 Cut remaining vegetables into 1-inch pieces and transfer to large bowl. Add tomatoes, beans, basil, and vinegar; stir to combine.

5 Meanwhile, remove chicken from marinade; discard marinade. Place chicken on grill rack and grill, turning often, until chicken is cooked through, 8–10 minutes. Transfer 3 chicken breasts to container; let cool. Cover and refrigerate up to 2 days for later use in Chicken Pan Bagnat, opposite. Serve remaining chicken breasts with ratatouille.

Per serving (1 chicken breast and 1 cup ratatouille): 329 Cal, 6 g Total Fat, 1 g Sat Fat, 0 g Trans Fat, 78 mg Chol, 450 mg Sod, 32 g Carb, 9 g Sugar, 12 g Fib, 39 g Prot, 109 mg Calc.

8 PointsPlus® value

FOR YOUR INFO
Serve the ratatouille with a vegetable salad made with baby spinach, sliced white mushrooms, thinly sliced red onions, red-wine vinegar, and salt and pepper to taste.

Chicken Pan Bagnat Serves 4 ⏱

2   **tablespoons red-wine vinegar**

2   **teaspoons olive oil**

1   **garlic clove, minced**

¼   **teaspoon pepper**

1   **(14-ounce) round whole wheat loaf bread**

3½ **cups reserved vegetables and 3 reserved chicken breasts, sliced, from Grilled Chicken with White Bean Ratatouille (opposite)**

▲ 1   **tomato, thinly sliced**

▲ 1   **cup arugula**

1   Whisk together vinegar, oil, garlic, and pepper in small bowl.

2   Using serrated knife, split loaf in half lengthwise, making bottom of loaf slightly thicker than top. Use your fingers to pull out and discard some of soft interior of bread (or save for making into breadcrumbs). Brush inside of loaf with half of vinegar mixture.

3   Cover bottom of bread with vegetables. Top with chicken, tomato, and arugula. Drizzle with remaining vinegar mixture. Cover with bread top and cut into 4 wedges.

Per serving (1 sandwich wedge): 367 Cal, 9 g Total Fat, 1 g Sat Fat, 0 g Trans Fat, 59 mg Chol, 486 mg Sod, 46 g Carb, 11 g Sugar, 11 g Fib, 31 g Prot, 55 mg Calc.

FOR YOUR INFO
If you have time, prepare the pan bagnat, wrap with plastic wrap, and refrigerate for 1 hour before serving to allow the flavors to blend.

Finish With: Honeyed Fruits with Toasted Almonds, page 130

Orange-Balsamic Glazed Chicken with Fennel and Carrots Serves 4 plus leftovers

2	teaspoons olive oil
2	shallots, minced
1/2	cup orange juice
1	tablespoon chopped fresh thyme or 1 teaspoon dried
2	tablespoons balsamic vinegar
1	tablespoon honey
▲ 2	fennel bulbs, trimmed, halved, and cut into 1 1/2-inch slices
▲ 2	carrots, sliced
▲ 3/4	cup reduced-sodium chicken broth
2	teaspoons grated orange zest
1/2	teaspoon salt
1/4	teaspoon pepper
▲ 7	(5-ounce) skinless boneless chicken breasts

1 Preheat oven to 350°F. Line large rimmed baking pan with foil.

2 Heat oil in large nonstick skillet over medium-high heat. Add shallots and cook, stirring often, until lightly browned, about 3 minutes. Add orange juice and thyme and bring to boil; cook, stirring occasionally, until liquid is reduced by about one half, about 2 minutes. Add vinegar and honey; cook 1 minute longer. Remove from heat and transfer glaze to small bowl.

3 Wipe out same skillet; spray with nonstick spray and set over medium-high heat. Add fennel and cook, turning often, until lightly browned, about 5 minutes. Add carrots and chicken broth; reduce heat, cover, and cook until vegetables are tender, about 12 minutes. Remove from heat and stir in orange zest and 1/4 teaspoon salt.

4 Transfer 1 cup of vegetable mixture to container and let cool. Cover and refrigerate for up to 4 days for later use in Chicken and Wheat-Berry Salad, opposite.

5 Meanwhile, place chicken in prepared baking pan. Sprinkle with pepper and remaining 1/4 teaspoon salt. Brush chicken breasts with glaze. Bake until chicken is cooked through, 12–14 minutes.

6 Transfer 3 chicken breasts to container and let cool. Cover and refrigerate up to 4 days for later use in Chicken and Wheat-Berry Salad, opposite. Serve remaining chicken breasts with vegetable mixture.

Per serving (1 chicken breast and about 3/4 cup vegetables): 245 Cal, 6 g Total Fat, 2 g Sat Fat, 0 g Trans Fat, 78 mg Chol, 309 mg Sod, 18 g Carb, 6 g Sugar, 4 g Fib, 31 g Prot, 76 mg Calc.

6 PointsPlus® value

Chicken and Wheat-Berry Salad Serves 4

▲ ½ **cup wheat berries**

▲ 1 **large navel orange**

1 **cup reserved fennel mixture, chopped, and 3 reserved chicken breasts, sliced, from** Orange-Balsamic Glazed Chicken with Fennel and Carrots **(opposite)**

▲ 3 **radishes, thinly sliced**

¼ **teaspoon salt**

▲ 4 **cups mixed salad greens**

1 Bring large pot of water to boil over medium-high heat; add wheat berries. Reduce heat and simmer, covered, until berries are tender but still chewy, 45 minutes–1 hour. Drain in colander and rinse under cold water; drain again.

2 With sharp knife, peel orange, removing all white pith. Working over large bowl, cut between membranes to release segments. Squeeze juice form membranes, then discard membranes. Add wheat berries, fennel mixture, chicken, radishes, and salt; toss gently to combine.

3 Divide greens among 4 plates. Top evenly with wheat-berry salad.

Per serving (generous 1 cup salad with 1 cup greens):
258 Cal, 4 g Total Fat, 1 g Sat Fat, 0 g Trans Fat, 59 mg Chol, 306 mg Sod, 30 g Carb, 7 g Sugar, 6 g Fib, 27 g Prot, 57 mg Calc.

6 PointsPlus® value

FOR YOUR INFO

To add more citrus flavor to the salad, add a pink grapefruit, cutting it into segments as directed for the orange in step 2.

Finish With: Peppered Strawberries with Yogurt, page 131

Cuban-Spiced Chicken Thighs with Red Beans and Rice
Serves 4 plus leftovers

3   **garlic cloves, halved**

▲ 1   **jalapeño, seeded**

1   **tablespoon fresh oregano or 1 teaspoon dried**

3   **tablespoons lime juice**

2   **tablespoons water**

1   **teaspoon ground cumin**

1   **teaspoon paprika**

7   **(1/4-pound) skinless boneless chicken thighs**

1   **tablespoon canola oil**

▲ 1   **small onion, finely chopped**

▲ 1   **Cubanelle pepper, diced**

▲ 1   **(14 1/2-ounce) can reduced-sodium chicken broth**

▲ 1 1/2   **cups quick-cooking brown rice**

▲ 1   **(15-ounce) can red kidney beans, rinsed and drained**

1/4   **cup chopped fresh cilantro**

1 Combine garlic, jalapeño, and oregano in food processor and pulse until finely chopped. Add lime juice, water, cumin, and paprika and process until well blended. Transfer to zip-close plastic bag; add chicken. Squeeze out air and seal bag; turn to coat chicken. Refrigerate, turning bag occasionally, at least 1 hour or overnight.

2 Remove chicken from marinade; discard marinade. Spray large nonstick ridged grill pan with nonstick spray and set over medium-high heat. Add chicken in batches, and cook, turning occasionally, until cooked through, about 12 minutes. Transfer 3 chicken thighs to container and let cool. Cover and refrigerate up to 4 days for later use in Chicken and Rice Burritos, opposite.

3 Meanwhile, heat oil over medium-high heat in large saucepan. Add onion and Cubanelle pepper; cook, stirring occasionally, until softened, about 5 minutes. Add broth, rice, and beans; bring to boil. Reduce heat, cover, and simmer until rice is tender, about 20 minutes. Remove from heat and let stand 5 minutes. Stir in cilantro.

4 Transfer 1 1/2 cups of rice mixture to container and let cool. Cover and refrigerate up to 4 days for later use in Chicken and Rice Burritos, opposite. Serve remaining chicken thighs with remaining rice mixture.

Per serving (1 chicken thigh and 3/4 cup bean and rice mixture): 368 Cal, 12 g Total Fat, 3 g Sat Fat, 0 g Trans Fat, 74 mg Chol, 95 mg Sod, 36 g Carb, 2 g Sugar, 8 g Fib, 29 g Prot, 35 mg Calc.

9 PointsPlus® value

FOR YOUR INFO
Cubanelle peppers are also known as banana peppers or Italian frying peppers. They are about 6 inches long and range in color from pale yellow to light green. If they are not available, you can use a small yellow or red bell pepper in this recipe.

Chicken and Rice Burritos Serves 4 🕐

1½ cups reserved rice mixture and 3 reserved chicken thighs, sliced, from **Cuban-Spiced Chicken Thighs with Red Beans and Rice (opposite)**

4 **(8-inch) fat-free whole wheat flour tortillas, warmed**

½ **cup shredded reduced-fat Mexican cheese blend**

▲ 1 **large tomato, diced**

1 Combine rice mixture and chicken thighs in medium microwavable dish; cover with wax paper. Microwave on High until heated through, 3–4 minutes.

2 Spoon one-fourth of rice mixture onto each tortilla; sprinkle evenly with cheese and tomato. Roll the tortilla up to enclose the filling.

Per serving (1 burrito): 414 Cal, 15 g Total Fat, 5 g Sat Fat, 0 g Trans Fat, 63 mg Chol, 646 mg Sod, 41 g Carb, 4 g Sugar, 10 g Fib, 28 g Prot, 324 mg Calc.

FOR YOUR INFO
To make the burritos more filling and flavorful, add some thinly sliced radishes and chopped fresh cilantro along with the tomato.

Pairs Well With: Lemony Spinach and Avocado Salad, page 86

Indian-Spiced Grilled Turkey Pitas Serves 4 plus leftovers

4	tablespoons lemon juice
1	tablespoon olive oil
2	teaspoons curry powder
1/2	teaspoon ground cumin
1/2	teaspoon salt
4	garlic cloves, minced
▲ 2	(3/4-pound) turkey tenderloins, cut into 1-inch pieces
▲ 1/2	cup plain fat-free Greek yogurt
2	tablespoons tahini
4	(6-inch) whole wheat pita breads, warmed
▲ 4	cups shredded romaine lettuce
▲ 1	large tomato, diced

1 Combine 3 tablespoons lemon juice, oil, curry powder, cumin, 1/4 teaspoon salt, and 3 garlic cloves in zip-close plastic bag; add turkey. Squeeze out air and seal bag; turn to coat turkey. Refrigerate, turning bag occasionally, at least 1 hour or up to 4 hours.

2 Whisk together yogurt, tahini, remaining 1 tablespoon lemon juice, remaining garlic clove, and remaining 1/4 teaspoon salt in medium bowl. Transfer 1/4 cup of yogurt sauce to container. Cover and refrigerate up to 4 days for later use in Turkey with Dal and Sweet Potatoes, opposite. Refrigerate remaining yogurt sauce until ready to serve.

3 Spray grill rack with nonstick spray and prepare medium-hot fire. Remove turkey from marinade; discard marinade. Thread turkey onto 8 (10-inch) metal skewers. Place skewers on grill rack and grill, turning occasionally, until cooked through, 12–14 minutes. Remove turkey from skewers. Transfer 2 cups of turkey to container and let cool. Cover and refrigerate up to 4 days for later use in Turkey with Dal and Sweet Potatoes, opposite.

4 Halve pita breads; fill each half evenly with remaining turkey, lettuce, and tomato. Drizzle evenly with remaining yogurt sauce.

Per serving (2 filled pita halves): 332 Cal, 7 g Total Fat, 1 g Sat Fat, 0 g Trans Fat, 34 mg Chol, 549 mg Sod, 42 g Carb, 3 g Sugar, 7 g Fib, 31 g Prot, 56 mg Calc.

FOR YOUR INFO
If you don't have metal skewers, you can use disposable wooden skewers, but remember to soak them in water for about 30 minutes before threading the turkey onto them to prevent them from burning on the grill.

Turkey with Dal and Sweet Potatoes Serves 4

- ▲ 1   **small onion, diced**
- 1   **garlic clove, minced**
- 1   **tablespoon grated peeled fresh ginger**
- 2   **teaspoon curry powder**
- ▲ 4   **cups reduced-sodium chicken broth**
- ▲ 1   **cup yellow lentils, picked over, rinsed, and drained**
- ▲ 1   **large sweet potato (³/₄-pound), peeled and cubed**
- 2   **cups reserved cooked turkey, chopped, and ¹/₄ cup reserved yogurt sauce from Indian-Spiced Grilled Turkey Pitas (opposite)**
- 2   **tablespoons chopped fresh cilantro**

1   Spray medium saucepan with nonstick spray and set over medium-high heat. Add onion and cook, stirring often, until softened and lightly browned, about 4 minutes. Add garlic, ginger, and curry powder; cook, stirring constantly, until fragrant, about 30 seconds.

2   Add broth and lentils and bring to boil. Reduce heat and simmer, covered, stirring occasionally, 15 minutes. Add sweet potato and simmer, covered, until lentils and sweet potato are tender, about 15 minutes.

3   Add turkey and cook just until heated through, about 3 minutes. Ladle dal evenly into 4 bowls; sprinkle with cilantro. Top evenly with yogurt sauce.

Per serving (1¹/₂ cups dal, 1 tablespoon yogurt sauce, and ¹/₂ tablespoon cilantro): 414 Cal, 10 g Total Fat, 2 g Sat Fat, 0 g Trans Fat, 62 mg Chol, 296 mg Sod, 45 g Carb, 6 g Sugar, 10 g Fib, 40 g Prot, 84 mg Calc.

FOR YOUR INFO

Dal is a traditional Indian dish made with dried lentils or peas.

Garlic-Parsley Salmon with Warm Tomato-Spinach Salad

Serves 4 plus leftovers

2	cups packed fresh flat-leaf parsley
3	garlic cloves, halved
1/4	cup water
2	tablespoons seasoned rice vinegar
2	tablespoons extra-virgin olive oil
1/2	teaspoon salt
1/4	teaspoon red pepper flakes
6	shallots, sliced
▲ 2	cups grape tomatoes
6	(6-ounce) salmon fillets
▲ 1	(7-ounce) bag baby spinach

1 To make garlic-parsley sauce, combine parsley, garlic, and water in food processor and pulse until finely chopped. Add vinegar, oil, 1/4 teaspoon salt, and pepper flakes; pulse until well combined. Transfer half (about 1/3 cup) of sauce to container; cover and refrigerate up to 4 days for later use in **Salmon and Pasta Salad with Summer Vegetables,** opposite.

2 Preheat oven to 425°F. Spray large rimmed baking pan with nonstick spray. Place shallots and tomatoes in baking pan; lightly spray with nonstick spray. Sprinkle with remaining 1/4 teaspoon salt; toss to coat. Bake until vegetables are lightly browned, stirring once, about 20 minutes.

3 Meanwhile, line a medium rimmed baking pan with foil; spray foil with nonstick spray. Place salmon in prepared pan. Brush with remaining garlic-parsley sauce. Bake until salmon is just opaque in center, about 10 minutes. Transfer 2 salmon fillets to container and let cool. Cover and refrigerate up to 4 days for later use in **Salmon and Pasta Salad with Summer Vegetables,** opposite.

4 Place spinach in large bowl; add hot roasted vegetables and toss to combine. Serve salmon with spinach mixture.

Per serving (1 salmon fillet and 1 1/2 cups salad): 382 Cal, 16 g Total Fat, 2 g Sat Fat, 0 g Trans Fat, 107 mg Chol, 329 mg Sod, 18 g Carb, 4 g Sugar, 4 g Fib, 42 g Prot, 105 mg Calc.

FOR YOUR INFO
To add even more flavor to the salad, add a handful of fresh mint, cilantro, or basil leaves along with the spinach.

Salmon and Pasta Salad with Summer Vegetables Serves 4 🕐

▲ 1 cup cherry or grape tomatoes, halved

▲ 1 small cucumber, peeled, seeded, and sliced

▲ 3 radishes, thinly sliced

1/3 cup reserved garlic-parsley sauce and 2 reserved salmon fillets, flaked, from **Garlic-Parsley Salmon with Warm Tomato-Spinach Salad (opposite)**

▲ 8 ounces whole wheat rotini or penne

▲ 1 ear corn on cob, kernels removed or 3/4 cup frozen corn kernels

1 Combine tomatoes, cucumber, radishes, and garlic-parsley sauce in large bowl; toss to coat. Let stand 15 minutes.

2 Meanwhile, cook pasta according to package directions, adding corn kernels during last 3 minutes of cooking time. Drain and rinse under cold running water. Drain again.

3 Add pasta mixture and salmon to tomato mixture; toss gently to combine.

Per serving (2 cups): 293 Cal, 6 g Total Fat, 1 g Sat Fat, 0 g Trans Fat, 0 mg Chol, 170 mg Sod, 53 g Carb, 5 g Sugar, 7 g Fib, 9 g Prot, 54 mg Calc.

FOR YOUR INFO

To make the salad more filling, serve it on a bed of mixed greens, baby arugula, or spinach.

Finish With: Browned Butter Pineapple Sundaes, page 131

Grilled Tuna and Vegetables with Caper Dressing Serves 4 plus leftovers

▲ 10   **small red potatoes, scrubbed (about 1 pound)**

▲ ½   **pound green beans, trimmed**

⅓   **cup lemon juice**

▲ 2   **tablespoons reduced-sodium chicken broth**

1   **tablespoon olive oil**

2   **tablespoons chopped fresh flat-leaf parsley**

1   **tablespoon capers, drained and minced**

1   **garlic clove, minced**

½   **teaspoon pepper**

¼   **teaspoon kosher salt**

▲ 6   **(5-ounce) tuna steaks, about 1¼-inch thick**

1   Place potatoes in steamer basket over 1-inch of boiling water; cover and steam 10 minutes. Add green beans to steamer basket; cover and steam until potatoes are tender, 5 minutes. Transfer 3 potatoes to container and let cool. Cover and refrigerate up to 4 days for later use in Tuna Niçoise Tartines, opposite. Let remaining potato mixture stand until cool enough to handle; slice potatoes.

2   Meanwhile, to make dressing, whisk together lemon juice, broth, oil, parsley, capers, garlic, pepper, and salt in small bowl. Transfer ¼ cup of dressing to container. Cover and refrigerate up to 4 days for later use in Tuna Niçoise Tartines, opposite.

3   Spray grill rack with nonstick spray and prepare medium-hot fire. Lightly spray tuna steaks with nonstick spray. Place tuna on grill rack and grill 2–3 minutes on each side for medium-rare or until desired doneness. Transfer 2 tuna steaks to container and let cool. Cover and refrigerate up to 4 days for later use in Tuna Niçoise Tartines, opposite.

4   Divide tuna steaks and potato mixture among 4 plates; drizzle evenly with reserved dressing.

Per serving (1 tuna steak, about 1 cup vegetables, and 1 tablespoon dressing): 428 Cal, 9 g Total Fat, 2 g Sat Fat, 0 g Trans Fat, 52 mg Chol, 166 mg Sod, 50 g Carb, 3 g Sugar, 6 g Fib, 38 g Prot, 49 mg Calc.

Tuna Niçoise Tartines Serves 4

▲ 1   **large egg**

   ¼   **cup reserved caper dressing, 3 reserved potatoes, thinly sliced, and 2 reserved tuna steaks, thinly sliced, from** Grilled Tuna and Vegetables with Caper Dressing **(opposite)**

   1   **teaspoon Dijon mustard**

▲ ¼   **cup diced red onion**

   ½   **cup fresh basil leaves**

   4   **(½-inch) slices whole wheat country-style bread, toasted (2 ounces each)**

▲ 2   **plum tomatoes, thinly sliced**

   1   **tablespoon chopped pitted Niçoise olives**

1   Place egg in small saucepan with enough water to cover; bring to boil. Cook 1 minute. Remove from heat. Cover and let stand 14 minutes. Drain and rinse under cold water. When cool enough to handle, remove shell. Chop egg.

2   Meanwhile, whisk together caper dressing and mustard in small bowl. Add onions; stir to coat.

3   Arrange basil leaves evenly on bread slices. Top evenly with sliced potatoes, half of dressing mixture, and tuna. Top with tomato slices; sprinkle with egg and olives. Top with remaining dressing mixture.

Per serving (1 open-face sandwich): 239 Cal, 7 g Total Fat, 2 g Sat Fat, 0 g Trans Fat, 80 mg Chol, 195 mg Sod, 24 g Carb, 3 g Sugar, 3 g Fib, 21 g Prot, 44 mg Calc.

6 PointsPlus® value

FOR YOUR INFO

Serve the sandwiches with a cucumber salad: Toss together a sliced English (seedless) cucumber, a small thinly sliced red onion, the zest and juice of 1 lemon, and salt and pepper to taste.

Finish With: Melon with Ginger-Lime Syrup, page 131

Seared Halibut with Quinoa-Cucumber Salad Serves 4 plus leftovers

▲ 1 1/3 cups quinoa

2 1/2 cups water

1 large shallot, chopped

3/4 teaspoon salt

3/4 teaspoon pepper

2 tablespoons chopped fresh dill

2 tablespoons chopped fresh mint

▲ 1/3 large English (seedless) cucumber, diced

2 tablespoons lemon juice

▲ 6 (5-ounce) halibut fillets

1 teaspoon smoked paprika

1 Place quinoa in medium saucepan and set over medium-high heat. Toast, stirring constantly, until lightly browned and fragrant, about 4 minutes. Carefully add water; stir in shallot, 1/2 teaspoon salt, and 1/2 teaspoon pepper. Bring to boil; reduce heat, cover, and simmer until quinoa is tender, about 12 minutes. Remove from heat and stir in dill and mint.

2 Transfer 1 1/2 cups quinoa mixture to container and let cool. Cover and refrigerate up to 4 days for later use in **Fish Cakes with Yogurt-Mint Sauce**, opposite. Stir cucumber and lemon juice into remaining quinoa.

3 Meanwhile, sprinkle halibut with paprika and remaining 1/4 teaspoon salt and 1/4 teaspoon pepper. Spray large nonstick skillet with nonstick cooking spray and set over medium-high heat. Add halibut and cook until just opaque in center, about 3 minutes on each side. Transfer 2 halibut fillets to container and let cool. Cover and refrigerate up to 4 days for later use in **Fish Cakes with Yogurt-Mint Sauce**, opposite.

4 Serve remaining halibut fillets with quinoa salad.

Per serving (1 halibut fillet and 1 cup salad): 232 Cal, 4 g Total Fat, 1 g Sat Fat, 0 g Trans Fat, 34 mg Chol, 262 mg Sod, 21 g Carb, 1 g Sugar, 2 g Fib, 27 g Prot, 75 mg Calc.

FOR YOUR INFO
To bulk up the quinoa salad, you can stir in 1 cup of halved grape tomatoes or 1 diced red bell pepper.

Fish Cakes with Yogurt-Mint Sauce Serves 4 🕐

½ cup plain fat-free Greek yogurt

½ cup diced cucumber

2 tablespoons lemon juice

2 tablespoons chopped fresh mint

1 garlic clove, minced

½ teaspoon sugar

¼ teaspoon pepper

1½ cups reserved quinoa mixture and 2 reserved halibut fillets, flaked, from **Seared Halibut with Quinoa-Cucumber Salad (opposite)**

4 scallions, thinly sliced

1 large egg white

¼ cup whole wheat flour

Flour for dusting

Lemon wedges

1 Stir together yogurt, cucumber, lemon juice, mint, garlic, sugar, and pepper in small bowl. Set aside.

2 Combine quinoa, halibut, scallions, egg white, and ¼ cup flour in large bowl; stir to mix well. Form mixture into 8 cakes (about ¼ cup each). Dust cakes lightly with flour.

3 Spray large nonstick skillet with nonstick spray and set over medium heat. Add fish cakes and cook until browned and heated through, 3–4 minutes on each side. Serve with yogurt sauce and lemon wedges.

Per serving (2 fish cakes and ¼ cup sauce): 257 Cal, 4 g Total Fat, 0 g Sat Fat, 0 g Trans Fat, 17 mg Chol, 160 mg Sod, 35 g Carb, 2 g Sugar, 4 g Fib, 21 g Prot, 86 mg Calc.

FOR YOUR INFO

If you have leftover mint from preparing this dish, add a sprig to a glass of iced tea, seltzer water, or plain water to make your beverage even more refreshing.

Pairs Well With: Buttered Broccoli with Lemon and Parmesan, page 36

Ginger Shrimp with Couscous and Vegetables Serves 4 plus leftovers

▲ 1   cup whole wheat
       couscous

▲ 2   carrots, thinly sliced

▲ ½   pound green beans,
       trimmed and halved

▲ 1   cup frozen shelled
       edamame

  1   tablespoon canola oil

▲ 6   scallions, thinly sliced

▲ 1½ pounds large peeled,
       deveined shrimp

  2   garlic cloves, minced

  1   tablespoon grated fresh
       peeled ginger

  ¼   cup lemon juice

  ½   teaspoon Asian (dark)
       sesame oil

  2   tablespoons chopped
       fresh cilantro

1   Cook couscous according to package directions.

2   Meanwhile, fill large saucepan three-quarters full with water. Set over high heat and bring to boil. Add carrots and cook 3 minutes. Add green beans and edamame; cook until vegetables are crisp-tender, about 5 minutes. Drain. Transfer 1 cup of vegetables to container and let cool. Cover and refrigerate up to 4 days for later use in Summer Garden Gazpacho with Shrimp, opposite.

3   Heat canola oil in large nonstick skillet over medium-high heat. Add scallions and cook, stirring constantly, 1 minute. Add shrimp, garlic, and ginger. Cook, stirring constantly, until shrimp are just opaque in center, about 4 minutes. Add lemon juice and sesame oil; cook, stirring constantly, 1 minute longer. Transfer 1 cup shrimp mixture to container and cool. Cover and refrigerate up to 4 days for later use in Summer Garden Gazpacho with Shrimp, opposite.

4   Fluff couscous with fork; transfer to large serving bowl. Add reserved vegetable mixture, shrimp mixture, and cilantro. Toss gently to combine.

Per serving (1½ cups): 266 Cal, 5 g Total Fat, 1 g Sat Fat, 0 g Trans Fat, 168 mg Chol, 213 mg Sod, 31 g Carb, 3 g Sugar, 7 g Fib, 25 g Prot, 90 mg Calc.

FOR YOUR INFO
Instead of the edamame, you can make this salad with frozen baby lima beans or frozen black-eyed peas.

Finish With: Orange-Glazed Tropical Fruits, page 131

Summer Garden Gazpacho with Shrimp Serves 4

- ▲ 2 **assorted-color bell peppers, diced**
- ▲ ½ **cucumber, peeled and diced**
- 3 **cups tomato juice**
- ▲ 2 **tomatoes, quartered**
- ▲ ½ **small red onion, sliced**
- 2 **garlic cloves, sliced**
- 3 **tablespoons red-wine vinegar**
- 1 **tablespoon olive oil**
- ¼ **teaspoon salt**
- ¼ **teaspoon black pepper**
- 1 **cup reserved shrimp, chopped, and 1 cup reserved vegetables, chopped, from Ginger Shrimp with Couscous and Vegetables (opposite)**

1 Place bell peppers and cucumber in large serving bowl; toss to combine. Puree 1 cup of bell pepper mixture and 1 cup of tomato juice in blender. Transfer pureed mixture to bowl with bell pepper mixture.

2 Puree remaining 2 cups tomato juice, tomatoes, onion, and garlic in blender. Add vinegar, oil, salt, and pepper; pulse until blended. Add to bowl and stir to mix well.

3 Cover and chill at least 1 hour or up to 4 hours. Top soup with shrimp and vegetables.

Per serving (1½ cups soup and about ½ cup shrimp and vegetable mixture): 196 Cal, 6 g Total Fat, 1 g Sat Fat, 0 g Trans Fat, 84 mg Chol, 386 mg Sod, 22 g Carb, 13 g Sugar, 5 g Fib, 13 g Prot, 79 mg Calc.

5 PointsPlus® value

Pasta with Asparagus, Zucchini, and Ricotta Serves 4 plus leftovers

▲ 8   **ounces whole wheat farfalle (bowtie) pasta**

▲ 1   **cup fat-free ricotta cheese**

2   **teaspoons grated lemon zest**

1   **tablespoon lemon juice**

1   **tablespoon olive oil**

6   **shallots, thinly sliced**

▲ 2   **zucchini, thinly sliced**

▲ 1   **pound asparagus, trimmed and cut into 2-inch pieces**

3   **garlic cloves, minced**

2   **teaspoons chopped fresh rosemary or 3/4 teaspoon dried**

1/2   **teaspoon salt**

1/4   **teaspoon pepper**

▲ 3/4   **cup reduced-sodium chicken broth**

2   **tablespoons chopped fresh chives**

1 Cook pasta according to package directions.

2 Meanwhile, stir together ricotta, lemon zest, and lemon juice in medium bowl. Transfer half of ricotta mixture (about 1/2 cup) to container. Cover and refrigerate up to 4 days for later use in Frittata Verde, opposite.

3 Heat oil in large nonstick skillet over medium-high heat. Add shallots and cook, stirring frequently, until softened, about 2 minutes. Add zucchini and asparagus and cook, stirring occasionally, until vegetables are crisp-tender, 7–8 minutes. Add garlic, rosemary, salt, and pepper; cook, stirring constantly, until fragrant, about 30 seconds. Transfer 2 cups of vegetable mixture to container and let cool. Cover and refrigerate up to 4 days for later use in Frittata Verde, opposite.

4 Add broth to remaining vegetables in skillet. Transfer vegetable mixture to large bowl. Add hot pasta and toss to combine. Divide pasta mixture among 4 plates; top evenly with reserved ricotta mixture and sprinkle with chives.

Per serving (2 cups pasta mixture and 2 tablespoons ricotta mixture): 296 Cal, 4 g Total Fat, 0 g Sat Fat, 0 g Trans Fat, 3 mg Chol, 218 mg Sod, 53 g Carb, 6 g Sugar, 7 g Fib, 15 g Prot, 156 mg Calc.

8 PointsPlus® value

FOR YOUR INFO
If you don't have chives on hand, sprinkle the pasta with thinly sliced scallion tops.

Frittata Verde Serves 4 🕐

2   teaspoons olive oil

▲ 3   scallions, chopped

2   cups reserved vegetables and ¹/₂ cup reserved ricotta mixture from Pasta with Asparagus, Zucchini and Ricotta (opposite)

¹/₄   teaspoon salt

¹/₄   teaspoon pepper

▲ 1   (16-ounce) carton fat-free egg substitute

1 Preheat oven to 375°F.

2 Heat oil in 10-inch ovenproof nonstick skillet over medium-high heat. Add scallions and cook, stirring occasionally, until softened, about 2 minutes. Stir in vegetables, salt, and pepper; cook, stirring occasionally, until heated through, 2 minutes.

3 Remove skillet from heat and pour egg substitute over vegetables. Drop ricotta mixture by rounded tablespoons onto egg substitute. Set skillet over medium-low heat and cook until frittata is almost set around edges, 3 minutes. Place skillet in oven and bake just until set in center, 15 minutes. Cut into 4 wedges.

Per serving (1 wedge): 139 Cal, 4 g Total Fat, 1 g Sat Fat, 0 g Trans Fat, 3 mg Chol, 521 mg Sod, 11 g Carb, 4 g Sugar, 2 g Fib, 17 g Prot, 181 mg Calc.

FOR YOUR INFO
You can add 2 cups chopped fresh spinach or arugula when you add the reserved vegetables in step 2.

Pairs Well With: Kale and Apple Salad, page 87

Roasted Spaghetti Squash with Pesto Vegetables Serves 4 plus leftovers

▲ 1   **(4-pound) spaghetti squash**

2   **teaspoons olive oil**

▲ 1   **sweet onion, chopped**

2   **garlic cloves, minced**

▲ 2   **cups broccoli florets**

▲ 1½   **cups cauliflower florets**

▲ ¼   **cup reduced-sodium chicken broth**

2   **tablespoons reduced-fat prepared basil pesto sauce**

1   **cup fat-free marinara sauce, warmed**

2   **tablespoons grated Parmesan cheese**

1 Preheat oven to 375°F. Cut squash in half lengthwise; remove and discard seeds. Place squash, cut side down, in medium rimmed baking pan. Bake until squash is tender, about 1 hour. Let cool 10 minutes. With fork, scrape squash into large bowl. Transfer 2 cups of squash to container and let cool. Cover and refrigerate for later use in Spaghetti Squash Pancakes with Yogurt, opposite.

2 Meanwhile, heat oil in large, deep nonstick skillet over medium-high heat. Add onion and cook, stirring often, until softened, 4 minutes. Add garlic and cook, stirring constantly, until fragrant, 30 seconds. Add broccoli, cauliflower, and broth. Cook, covered, until vegetables are crisp-tender, 6–8 minutes. Add pesto and stir to combine.

3 Divide remaining spaghetti squash evenly among 4 plates. Top evenly with vegetable mixture and marinara sauce. Sprinkle with Parmesan cheese.

Per serving (1 cup spaghetti squash, ³/₄ cup vegetable mixture, ¼ marinara sauce, and 1½ teaspoons cheese): 213 Cal, 6 g Total Fat, 1 g Sat Fat, 0 g Trans Fat, 4 mg Chol, 424 mg Sod, 34 g Carb, 12 g Sugar, 8 g Fib, 8 g Prot, 172 mg Calc.

5 PointsPlus® value

FOR YOUR INFO

In Japan, spaghetti squash is called "gold string melon" and its cooked flesh lives up to the name, looking like thin golden strings.

Spaghetti Squash Pancakes with Yogurt
Serves 4

2 cups reserved cooked spaghetti squash from Roasted Spaghetti Squash with Pesto Vegetables **(opposite)**

▲ **1** large egg white

1 shallot, finely chopped

¼ cup whole wheat flour

1 teaspoon chopped fresh thyme

¼ teaspoon salt

¼ teaspoon pepper

▲ **4** tablespoons plain fat-free Greek yogurt

1 Stir together spaghetti squash, egg white, shallot, flour, thyme, salt, and pepper in large bowl. Shape mixture into pancakes, using 2 heaping tablespoons for each pancake.

2 Spray large nonstick skillet with nonstick spray and set over medium-high heat. Add pancakes in two batches and cook until browned and heated through, 3–4 minutes on each side. Serve pancakes with yogurt.

Per serving (3 pancakes and 1 tablespoon yogurt): 87 Cal, 2 g Total Fat, 0 g Sat Fat, 0 g Trans Fat, 54 mg Chol, 190 mg Sod, 15 g Carb, 4 g Sugar, 3 g Fib, 5 g Prot, 46 mg Calc.

FOR YOUR INFO
Cooked spaghetti squash freezes very well. When you have extra, place individual servings of it in zip-close freezer bags and freeze. To defrost, simply plunge frozen bags into hot water for a few minutes until thawed.

Pairs Well With: Quinoa Pilaf with Tomatoes and Spinach, page 181

Cilantro Pesto–Grilled Vegetables and Pasta Serves 4 plus leftovers

▲ 2   **red bell peppers, quartered lengthwise**

▲ 2   **large yellow squash, cut lengthwise into thick slices**

▲ 2   **large zucchini, cut lengthwise into thick slices**

▲ 1   **large red onion, cut into ¼-inch slices**

▲ 8   **ounces whole wheat spaghetti**

¼   **cup prepared cilantro or basil pesto sauce**

▲ ¼   **cup reduced-sodium chicken broth**

¼   **cup crumbled reduced-fat feta cheese**

1   Spray grill rack with nonstick spray and prepare medium-hot fire.

2   Place bell peppers, yellow squash, zucchini, and onion in large bowl; lightly spray with nonstick spray. Place vegetables on grill rack and grill, turning often, until lightly browned and crisp-tender, 8–10 minutes. Transfer to cutting board; cut into 1-inch pieces. Transfer 2 cups of grilled vegetables to container and let cool. Cover and refrigerate up to 4 days for later use in Grilled Vegetable–Pesto Pizza, opposite.

3   Cook pasta according to package directions; transfer to large serving bowl. Add reserved vegetables, pesto, and broth; toss to combine. Sprinkle with feta cheese.

Per serving (1¾ cup pasta mixture and 1 tablespoon cheese): 335 Cal, 9 g Total Fat, 2 g Sat Fat, 0 g Trans Fat, 8 mg Chol, 273 mg Sod, 53 g Carb, 8 g Sugar, 11 g Fib, 15 g Prot, 116 mg Calc.

9 PointsPlus® value

FOR YOUR INFO
Look for cilantro pesto in gourmet grocery stores. If you can't find it, you can use basil pesto and the recipe will still be delicious.

Finish With: Nectarines with Raspberry Yogurt Sauce, page 130

Grilled Vegetable–Pesto Pizza Serves 4

Cornmeal for
sprinkling pan

1 (15-ounce) package
refrigerated or thawed
frozen whole wheat
pizza dough

4 tablespoons prepared
cilantro or basil pesto
sauce

▲ 1 large tomato, thinly
sliced

2 cups reserved grilled
vegetables from
Cilantro Pesto–Grilled
Vegetables and Pasta
(opposite)

¹⁄₂ cup shredded part-skim
mozzarella cheese

1 Spray large baking pan with nonstick spray and sprinkle
lightly with cornmeal.

2 Divide dough evenly into 4 pieces. With floured hands,
gently stretch and shape each piece of dough into 4 x 8-inch
rectangle. Place on prepared baking pan; cover loosely with
plastic wrap and let rise in warm spot 30 minutes.

3 Preheat oven to 450°F. Spread pesto evenly on pizza doughs,
leaving ¹⁄₂-inch border around edges. Top evenly with tomato
slices and grilled vegetables. Bake 7 minutes. Sprinkle pizzas
evenly with mozzarella and bake until cheese is melted and
crust is lightly browned, 5–6 minutes longer.

Per serving (1 pizza): 421 Cal, 13 g Total Fat, 3 g Sat Fat,
0 g Trans Fat, 13 mg Chol, 693 mg Sod, 60 g Carb, 9 g Sugar,
10 g Fib, 16 g Prot, 215 mg Calc.

FOR YOUR INFO
Save time by using a thin prebaked whole wheat pizza crust
instead of dough in this recipe and reduce the baking time by
2–3 minutes.

Recipes by *PointsPlus* value

Tuscan-Style Beef Roast with Fennel and Olives, 18

Recipes that work with the Simply Filling technique

Cincinnati-Style Beef Chili, 80

Index

Dry and Liquid Measurement Equivalents

If you are converting the recipes in this book to metric measurements, use the following chart as a guide.

TEASPOONS	TABLESPOONS	CUPS	FLUID OUNCES
3 teaspoons	1 tablespoon		1/2 fluid ounce
6 teaspoons	2 tablespoons	1/8 cup	1 fluid ounce
8 teaspoons	2 tablespoons plus 2 teaspoons	1/6 cup	
12 teaspoons	4 tablespoons	1/4 cup	2 fluid ounces
15 teaspoons	5 tablespoons minus 1 teaspoon	1/3 cup minus 1 teaspoon	
16 teaspoons	5 tablespoons plus 1 teaspoon	1/3 cup	
18 teaspoons	6 tablespoons	1/4 cup plus 2 tablespoons	3 fluid ounces
24 teaspoons	8 tablespoons	1/2 cup	4 fluid ounces
30 teaspoons	10 tablespoons	1/2 cup plus 2 tablespoons	5 fluid ounces
32 teaspoons	10 tablespoons plus 2 teaspoons	2/3 cup	
36 teaspoons	12 tablespoons	3/4 cup	6 fluid ounces
42 teaspoons	14 tablespoons	1 cup minus 2 tablespoons	7 fluid ounces
45 teaspoons	15 tablespoons	1 cup minus 1 tablespoon	
48 teaspoons	16 tablespoons	1 cup	8 fluid ounces

VOLUME

1/4 teaspoon	1 milliliter
1/2 teaspoon	2 milliliters
1 teaspoon	5 milliliters
1 tablespoon	15 milliliters
2 tablespoons	30 milliliters
3 tablespoons	45 milliliters
1/4 cup	60 milliliters
1/3 cup	80 milliliters
1/2 cup	120 milliliters
2/3 cup	160 milliliters
3/4 cup	175 milliliters
1 cup	240 milliliters
1 quart	950 milliliters

LENGTH

1 inch	25 millimeters
1 inch	2.5 centimeters

WEIGHT

1 ounce	30 grams
1/4 pound	120 grams
1/2 pound	240 grams
1 pound	480 grams

OVEN TEMPERATURE

250°F	120°C	400°F	200°C
275°F	140°C	425°F	220°C
300°F	150°C	450°F	230°C
325°F	160°C	475°F	250°C
350°F	180°C	500°F	260°C
375°F	190°C	525°F	270°C

Note: Measurement of less than 1/8 teaspoon is considered a dash or a pinch.
Metric volume measurements are approximate.